HOW HOCKEY SAVED
A JEW
FROM THE HOLACAUST:
The Rudi Ball Story
By
J. Wayne Frye

TO: My California Lutheran University hockey teams from 1986-1992. Playing before standing room only crowds all those years, they are still a favourite topic of California hockey lovers who fondly recall "Thunder on Ice." It was indeed a privilege to be called "coach" by these young men. Although I have coached many players before and after "Thunder on Ice," I have never had a group of people more determined and driven then these players, and they did it all for me. It is a memory I shall always cherish. *JWF*

Catalogue Number: 20116196107

ISBN: 978-0-9735973-7-0 (Peninsula Publishing)

Produced Under Licence From Fireside Books

Peninsula Publishing
Distributed by
Educational Research Associates

The Rudi Ball Story

Table of Contents

Prologue: The Boundaries That Would Enslave Us	7
Chapter 1: The Whirlwind	10
Chapter 2: A Legendary Friendship	23
Chapter 3: The Gathering Storm	31
Chapter 4: Crumbling the Walls of Tyranny	35
Chapter 5: Standing Tall Against the Winds of Tyranny	47
Chapter 6: Today is Our Day, Not Yours	54
Chapter 7: There is Blood on the Battlefield	66
Epilogue: It Saved Me From the Holocaust	80
Statistical Information on Rudi Ball	84
Addendum – Newspaper Article	85
Photo Credits/Bibliographic Information	94
Vocabulary/Chapter Questions	106

For Readers Outside Canada:
Please note all words are spelled using the Canadian dictionary, so USA/UK/Australian/European teachers should explain the different spellings to their students

"Hockey is a form of disorderly conduct in which the score is kept." Doug Larson

"Hockey players wear numbers, because you can't always identify the body by dental records." Author Unknown

"Hockey is figure skating in a war zone." Author Unknown

"When hell freezes over, I'll play hockey there, too." Author Unknown

"I'm really no different from anybody else, except sometimes I get my name I the paper." Bobby Orr

"Every day is a great day for hockey." Mario Lemeiux

"How would you like a job where every time you make a mistake, a big red light goes on and 18,000 people boo." Jacques Plante – Goalie

"Hit somebody - anybody." Gordie Howe

"Hockey is a fast body contact game played with a club in your hand and knives laced to your feet." Paul Calico

**ABOUT THE INSPIRATION FOR
THE BOOK
CLU THUNDER ON ICE**
1986-1992 (See Next Page for More Players)

**SOME OF THE PLAYERS
AND THEIR UNIQUE NAMES**
Jeff "Piledriver" Phillips, Stan "Slammer" Smidt, Bret "Hodad" Hardinson, Alec "A Bomb" Arho, Chad "Minuteman" Nelson, Greg "TNT" Landrum, Kevin "Cobra" Gould, Jorn "The Hulk" Huseby, Lance "Lightning" Bartlett, Scott "Scruff" Klein, Richard "Madman" Mack, Derek "Demon" Greenlea, Ove "Overdrive" Ness, Truls "Slasher" Midtbo, Won "The Wind" Yi, Scott, "Dirtbag" Myers, John "Jammer" Devries, Thomas "Pretty Boy" Patay, Wade "Wammer" Bradison, Oyvind "Hitman" Helgesen, Matt "The Goon" Groff, Grif "Bad Boy" Boyster, (Coach Wayne "The Hammer" Frye). **Not pictured players:** Paavo "Speedy" Salmi, Tapio "Tornado" Rantannen. Not pictured staff: <u>Solveig Langeland & Shelly N. Froyd – Marketing Managers.</u>

THUNDER ON ICE
The Team

1988-1992

Pictured above, centre, is the author of this book with his undefeated 1990 California Lutheran University hockey team. All 38 players from 1986-1992 were the inspiration for this book. Having one of the most diverse teams in the history of university hockey (players from European countries, Asia, Canada and the USA, representing a variety of ethnic backgrounds, and the first college hockey player with Cystic Fibrosis), the camaraderie of these young men led Wayne Frye to research similar teams. While doing so, he came across the story of Rudi Ball and the 1936 German hockey team that stood by their fellow player against the evil of Adolph Hitler. Over 20 years after his initial research, he has written a riveting account of this extraordinary player and his team-mates who refused to bend before the winds of tyranny that blew across Germany at the time.

PROLOGUE
THE BOUNDARIES THAT WOULD ENSLAVE US

MY DAD AND THE GAME
by
Ryan D. Frye

I remember the trips, the falls and all the pain.
I would be a runaway train.
The voice I heard would stay the same.
Go out, give it your all and assume no blame,
For it is the name of the game.

Then, I would come off the ice,
Look at my dad with a knowing smile,
Seeing approval in his glinting eyes,
That it was our way of delivering the pain,
For the sake of a beautiful game.

Hockey is a war that is waged between opposing forces in an area that measures 85 X 200 Feet (26 X 61 Metres) or 98 X 200 Feet (30 X 61 Metres). The beauty of it can only be experienced by those who truly understand emancipation and liberation. As my daughter Andrea once told me when she was only 9, "Dad, hockey is freedom. When I am accelerating down the ice, the cold air slapping me in the face, I am truly free. It is like I am flying and have wings."

My son Ken, who never exhibited any anger, no matter what offence opposing players perpetrated against him, was playing a game in an antiquated arena in West Covina, California in the 1980's. The side boards had no plexi-glass and were a mere one metre high (about three feet). An opposing player delivered a devastating check that sent him reeling over the boards into a large trash can. With his feet sticking straight up in the air, the silver blades of his skates flickering in the dim light, I could not help but laugh as he struggled to get out of the trash can. After the game, he went over to the opposing player who had delivered the check and said, "nice check, man. I never dreamed I would end up in a garbage can when I started playing hockey."

When the puck is dropped, two teams spend an hour in a titanic struggle of immovable forces against unstoppable objects. Yet, when the game is over, players line-up and shake hands, as there are no winners or losers as long as both sides know they gave it their all. I used to tell my players on the university hockey teams I coached, "as long as the opposing team knows they were in a battle, the scoreboard does not always reflect the effort each player puts forth. If you can skate off the ice, secure in the knowledge that you expended your maximum effort, you will never be a loser, regardless of what the scoreboard reads."

In 1991, my team played in the Pacific Collegiate Hockey Association championship game against a talented Cal Tech team. In the first period, my two star players were knocked out of the game with injuries. Although we lost the game 2-1, the drive and determination displayed by the 20 players that day makes it the single greatest game I ever coached, because I have never seen a more courageous effort on a hockey rink by a dedicated group of young men. Unfortunately, we are not all born with the genes that make us great athletes. However, we are all born with the ability to face adversity and overcome it. Hockey is a metaphor for life. We cannot always be winners, but we can always make an effort.

This is the story of a great athlete, but it also the story of lesser skilled players who stood shoulder to shoulder with their talented team-mate and refused to give into tyranny. Above all, this is the story of a game, and how this game transcends the boundaries imposed by those who would enslave us.   JWF

CHAPTER 1
THE WHIRLWIND

On March 27, 1910 the Berlin winter was still raging, as a heavy snow fell across most of Germany. A faint cry in the downtown hospital signalled the arrival of Rudolph Victor Ball. Rudi's older brothers, Gerhard and Heinz, thought he appeared to be a little scrawny, and laughed when they looked at their new brother wrapped comfortably in his mother's arms. Yet, this scrawniest of the Ball brothers would emerge as the premiere European hockey player of his time, and he would use those skills to survive the Holocaust, while other Jews were being gassed in concentration camps all across Europe.

The Berlin of Rudi's youth was a vibrant and energetic city that attracted people from all over Europe to what was at the time, the most exciting city in Europe. The pace of change was greater than any other place in the world, and there was always something exciting going on. Yet, just like the world of today, there was a great economic gap between the haves and have-nots.

Meat-packing was the biggest industry in the city, and those who worked in the slaughter-houses and packing companies were forced to toil for low wages and live in dilapidated tenements. Like today's capitalistic societies, immigrants provided the labour that oiled the wheels of industry. Yet, only a kilometre (approximately 3/5's of a mile) away from these squalid areas, were the magnificent estates of the tycoons who reaped obscene profits by exploiting cheap labour. Even the Kaiser's palace was within walking distance of these monuments to human misery that stood as a testament to greed.

Rudi's family was what would be considered by today's standards, upper middle class. He lived in a nice flat near the meat-packing plants, but was sheltered from the abject poverty that was so prevalent in the tenements. He was in an area of the city that consisted of the Jewish professional class that specialized in everything from operating pastry shops to making custom home furnishings. This was a time when artisans (people who worked with their hands) were highly valued and respected for their abilities, unlike today's world where those who shuffle money around from one nefarious endeavour to another are highly valued and reap the most outlandish salaries and perks. Unfortunately, like today's governments, the German government was more concerned with rewarding those at the top than helping those at the bottom. Like most children, Rudi was unaware of the poverty that was around him, and of the great suffering of those who had to scrounge for their daily bread.

Berlin Centre City as it Appeared in 1910
When Rudi Ball Was Born

**Kaiser Wilhelm's Palace Was Only
A Few Blocks From the Slums of Berlin.
The Ruling Classes had no Concern
For Those Who Were not
Born into Power and Privilege.**

Germany was becoming the most powerful nation in the world, but it had deep social divisions. While lavish amounts were spent on the military, social amenities were almost non-existent. Out of this great disparity between the haves and have-nots, social movements developed and the most powerful revolutionary political party representing the workers at the time was founded, the German Social Democratic Party. With the growing disparity of income, the seeds of discontent were being sown. A plea for fairness was being heard, and the people were growing restless, so a conscious effort was made by those in power to instil fear of outsiders in the populace. Intense militarization was laying the groundwork for World War I, which would be lost by Germany and lead to the rise of Adolph Hitler and the Nazis.

Slums Like These Were Within Walking Distance of Kaiser Wilhelm's Palace. Just Like Today's World, There Was a Great Disparity Between the Rich and the Poor

Germany was ruled by Kaiser Wilhelm during the early 1900's. It was he who led his countrymen into World War I as an ally of the Austro-Hungarian Empire, after the assassination of Archduke Ferdinand. When he announced from his palace balcony that the nation was going to war, the entire city was filled with exhilaration for what was considered a noble cause. Even the socialists, and the Association of German Jews, were enthusiastically behind the war effort.

The war, that most assumed would only last a few months, dragged on for four years. As the death toll mounted, the people of Germany grew weary of the cause. The press, primarily run by Jews, began to attack the military and the Kaiser for leading the nation into the folly of an un-winnable war. This led to a growing animosity between the government and the Jewish population.

Food became so scarce that Berliners would slaughter horses in the streets and cut up their carcasses to feed their starving families. Animals in the Berlin zoo were used for food, and toward the end of the war the worst flu epidemic in history swept through Germany, killing an average of 2,000 people a day. Finally, the residents of Berlin forced the Kaiser to flee the country.

When the war ended in 1918, Rudi was 8 years old. As a young boy, he saw first hand the results of the Treaty of Versailles that ended the war. The victorious allies (principally Great Britain, France, Australia, Canada and the USA) forced such harsh terms on the German's that the seeds of economic destruction were sown that would lead the German people to blame the Jews for the loss of the war and usher in the conditions that would see the Germans turn to a messiah-like orator named Adolph Hitler to return them to their former glory. Hitler was a master of fear, and he used fear to make the German people believe all his acts of aggression were not war, but ways of protecting the people.

The so-called "guilt clause" of the Treaty of Versailles placed full blame for the war on Germany and ordered reparations (payments) of 132 billion German marks (roughly 500 billion dollars in 2011 U.S. dollars) be made to the allies. This debt fed a cycle of hyperinflation (rapidly increasing prices for goods that are needed for survival) that pushed Germany to the brink of financial collapse. In 1920, the German Duetsche Mark stood at 99 to the U.S. dollar. In 1921, it was 263 to the U.S. dollar. By 1922 it was 7,368 to the dollar. In 1923 it was 4,210,500,000,000 to the dollar. It took Germany until 2010 to finally pay off the debt forced on it by the Treaty of Versailles. This debt and the hyperinflation that resulted from the terms imposed on Germany fed the feelings of resentment toward the allies, and would eventually catapult Hitler to power. Just as in today's world, many of the seeds for future wars are sowed by an unwillingness to be gracious in victory. The allies refused to offer the hand of compassion and the world paid for the price.

**People Lining Up for Bread Distribution in 1923
(It took a wheelbarrow full of
German marks for one loaf.)**

Like most children, Rudi and his brothers were somewhat oblivious to this suffering, as children always seem to find time for frivolity no matter how dire the circumstances of their existence. While this economic and political disaster was unfolding, young Rudi loved to play in the streets of Berlin with his older brothers. However, he was often left out of athletic contests, as he was puny, and assumed, by his brothers, to be somewhat of a burden. While his brothers, Gerhard and Heinz spent hours using an old can top and broom sticks to play street hockey, Rudi would nonchalantly sit on the curb cheering them on. When his brothers eventually started playing on ice, Rudi seemed disinterested. Rather than watching his brother Heinz push around a rubber disc with a stick while gliding effortlessly on the ice, or his brother Gerhard keep the disc out of the mesh net with daring moves in goal, he preferred the company of his mother.

As a child, Rudi was rather precocious around the house. Yet, he was shy in the presence of everyone but his family, and was, no doubt, a mama's boy. He clung desperately to his mother around
strangers, often hiding behind her dress when she would stop and talk to people on the streets of Berlin. There seems to be no direct evidence to prove it, but he was probably his mother's favourite.

A child identifies with the things, images and words surrounding him. For Rudi, those images and words became increasingly anti-Jewish, as the economic peril of Germany made the Jews easy targets for those who needed someone to blame for the societal turmoil caused by the loss of World War I. Yet, it appears in his youth, Rudi was not overtly aware of what was beginning to manifest itself in a society that was headed for destruction and evil of the vilest form. Considered part of the bourgeois class (those who controlled the wealth), Rudi's parents would eventually become targets of the Nazi's, who would paint all Jews as leeches who preyed on the less fortunate. Yet, for much of his youth, Rudi was spared overt acts of discrimination, as he appeared to lead a somewhat isolated existence in the Jewish section of Berlin.

In order to put Rudi's childhood in the proper context, one must also understand the social upheavals that were taking place in Germany at this time. In 1919, Anton Dexler formed the German Workers' Party to fight against what he called a deterioration of German will and the destruction of the social fabric. One of its first members and the eventual leader was Adolph Hitler. Upon becoming leader in 1920, he immediately renamed the party the National Socialist German Workers' Party (Nazis) and defined the allies, the Versailles Treaty, the communists and the Jews as the cause of all Germany's problems.

After a failed attempt to takeover the Bavarian government in 1923, Hitler and several other prominent Nazis were sent to prison for treason. There, he wrote *Mein Kampf* (*My Struggle*), which advocated the following:

(1)   National Socialism – loyalty to Germany, racial purity, equality and state control of the economy.
(2)   Racism - the triumph of the Aryan race by armed force, because all races, especially Jews, were inferior to the Aryan (pure German) "Master Race."
(3)   Lebensraum – to expand into Poland and Russia to get living space.
(4)   Strong Government – complete obedience to the Fuhrer (leader).

**The Below Photo Illustrates One of the Reasons
for Hitler's Rise to Power.
(The German mark was so useless that people
were using them in place of firewood.)**

As Hitler's influence was growing, Rudi was maturing. He was an excellent student and showed great promise as a scholar. While his brothers were honing their hockey skills and making names for themselves throughout Germany, Rudi had little interest in hockey. In fact, he rarely went to see his brothers play. Most of his time was devoted to his studies, until one day in 1925, when at the age of 15, he decided to go with some friends to a nearby outdoor ice rink.

Outdoor Rink (1925)

On this day, there was a game between Berliner SC and Weiner EV. Blake Watson, a Canadian medical student was on one of the teams. He had played on a Memorial Cup winning team from Manitoba with several other players who wound up in the NHL. Rudi could not take his eyes off the fleet-footed Canadian. As he watched Watson play, he reflected back on his brothers, who by now were legitimate German hockey stars and thought that the sport didn't really look all that difficult. Although he was only 5:4 (162.5 Centimetres) and weighed a mere 140 pounds (63 Kilograms), he noticed that the really good skaters avoided getting hit by using superior skating skills. These men were impressive in their uniforms, and were actually playing with a real rubber puck, rather than the wooden ones that children were forced to play with in the streets of Berlin.

This would be Rudi's coming out, because before he had only watched his brothers and occasionally played when there was no one else available to even up the teams. For some reason, he was fascinated by the rubber disc, as he thought it much better than the wooden ones that were always coming apart just when you were about to take a shot.

**Rudi's First Pucks Were Wood Scraps From a
Furniture Plant Because Rubber Pucks
Were too Expensive**

Rudi had tried skating several times, and his father had even bought him an expensive pair of Canadian skates. Yet, he rarely skated, because he had weak ankles. However, he had watched his brothers and had received some instruction from an old Swedish hockey player, Nils Molander, who lived in Germany.

Strapping on his expensive Canadian skates, he joined a

game of pick-up hockey among several senior league players that day. As the game progressed, Rudi seemed to effortlessly glide up and down the ice, skating fearlessly around the other players and easily flipping the wooden disc into the net. It appeared no one was capable of catching him or prying him loose from the puck, as his stick handling was superb. Many years later, he would say that he had simply watched his brothers Heinz and copied his moves.

People standing alongside the rink became fascinated with what was occurring. It appeared that this young man was elastic, as when hit, he would simply bounce back up in stride, continuing to skate toward the net, stick handling with the grace of an artist putting brush strokes on a painting. His skates were like glue, sticking to the ice, as he skated around with a broad smile on his face. All this from a young man, who had never really seriously considered playing organized hockey. If the phrase "a natural" ever applied to anyone, it was certainly appropriate for young Rudi Ball. Before long, a few hockey officials, while observing the young man's on-ice display of superior skills, were huddling to discuss the prowess displayed by this remarkable athlete who had caught the attention all present that day.

Soon afterward, Rudi joined a league team. Always in awe of his brothers, he was extremely surprised when he became the Ball brother who was the most honoured hockey player in German history.

One of the sport officials who observed the magnificent display of stick handling, shooting and skating by Rudi said "that kid is a skating whirlwind."

Rudi's Canadian Made Skates

CHAPTER 2
A LEGENDARY FRIENDSHIP

The emergence of Rudi as a hockey player coincided with the rise of Nazism in Germany. It could be considered somewhat ironic that just as Hitler was beginning to spread his vile doctrine of hate and blame on the Jews, that the soon-to-be best hockey players in Germany (Heinz Ball, Gerhard Ball and Rudi Ball) were all Jewish.

In 1924, after serving only nine months of his five year sentence, Hitler was released from Landsberg prison. His book, *Mein Kampf*, was being read by those who felt that most of the nation's problems were being caused by outside sources (the former allied countries) and the wealthy German Jews. It could be argued that in one respect Hitler was correct; many problems related to poverty are indeed caused by the concentration of wealth in the hands of the few. That is as true today, as it was in 1920's Germany. However, Hitler heaped all the blame on the Jews, whom he saw as the moneyed class, when, in reality, the majority of the Jews suffered in poverty as did most other Germans.

It is always convenient to have an enemy to rally people to support your cause. Whether it is Jews, Blacks, Gypsies, homosexuals, communists, socialists, Muslims or some other group, pointing the finger of condemnation is a tried and true method to get people to support a cause. "They want to destroy our way of life" or "they are after us," is a refrain used by those who can always find a scapegoat for the serious issues facing society. In reality, the real problems are generally caused by a lack of thoughtful reflection and compassion on the part of those who had rather lay blame than genuinely tackle problems.

For the 1927-1928 season, Rudi tried out for and made the second tier Berlin SC Brandenburg team. He was quick, elegant, had incredible speediness and was a magician with the stick. As a right
winger, he led his team in assists, goals and total points. His lighting-fast release made his shots accurate, and as the smallest player on the team, his cleaver skating ability and determination made him a crowd favourite.

In the 1928-1929 season he was promoted to Berliner SC Tier 1, where he joined his brothers Heinz and Gerhard. The team won the first of six straight German championships that year, and went on to win eight championships in 10 years.

Rudi was perennially the best player on the team. In his first championship game (1929), Rudi scored the game-winning goal in the third period as Berliner SC defeated their most truculent rival, SC Riessersee 2-1 in a game before a huge crowd in downtown Berlin.

In 1929, the brothers appeared in their first international game at the Berlin Sportpalast Arena, where a capacity crowd saw them literally destroy the British Collegiate champions, Oxford University, 6-0. Gerhard was superior in goal and Rudi had two goals, while Heinz delivered some devastating checks and racked up two assists as all three of them electrified the standing room only crowd, bringing them to their feet to cheer for the three Ball brothers. This was also the first of many times that their father and mother would enthusiastically sit in the stands at international games to proudly cheer on their now famous sons.

At the age of 18, Rudi was selected for the 1929 European All-Star Team that played a series of games throughout Europe against other teams, including an all-star team from Germany. He would continue to be selected as a European All-Star throughout his illustrious career.

In these all-star games, Rudi played alongside some of the greatest European players of all time, including Herbert Bruck (Austria), Bibi Torriani (Switzerland) and Joseph Malecek (Czechoslovakia). This was an incredibly potent all-star team that was literally unstoppable, and they performed incredible feats on the ice rink that are still talked about today in Europe.

Fortunately, Rdi's line-mate on the All Star team was fellow Berliner SC player, Gustav Jaenecke (Germany), who was the friend who would help insure Rudi's inclusion on the German teams that Hitler insisted exclude Jews, because of what he termed racial inferiority. They were a pair on the ice that struck fear into the hearts of opponents. Their friendship would become legend in the annals of sports, as it would show the power of those who are willing to stand against the evils of prejudice.

While Rudi was enjoying great success in hockey, the seeds of discontent were being sown as a result of dire economic conditions that were being exploited by Hitler and the Nazi party. The scapegoat for these ills was the Jews of Germany.

**The Below Chart Illustrates
The Unemployment Situation By Years**

DATE	% UNEMPLOYED
1928	4%
1929	9%
1930	16%
1931	19%
1932	24%
1933	30%

Although the severe persecution of the Jews was still a few years away, as early as 1923, with the publication of *Mein Kampf*, the Jewish Germans were being targeted by the more antagonistic Nazis and their followers as the causes of the economic maladies the country was undergoing.

While Hitler was stirring up the German population with his rousing oratorical skills, Rudi and his brothers were arousing crowds with masterful accomplishments on the ice. In 1930, the three brothers had an incredible season and led the team to a rout of TSV Brandenburg in the German championship game by a score of 9-1, with Rudi scoring three goals and garnering one assist. In the three game championship series that year, Rudi scored a total of eight goals.

The first world hockey championship was played in 1930 at Chamonix, France. The tournament was somewhat unusual, as the extraordinarily skilled Canadian team was considered the best in the world, and the tournament was intended to decide who would Canada in the Gold Medal Game. Since Canada was only required to participate in the championship game, they elected to play two exhibition games as tune-ups. They defeated Czechoslovakia 14-1 in Berlin, but ironically, when they played Austria in a raging snow storm in downtown Vienna, the Austrians won 1-0. The loss to Austria was the first time any Canadian team had ever lost to a European team.

**Poster for the 1930 World Championships
In Chamonix, France**

Meanwhile, Germany won all four of its games in the tournament for the right to meet Canada in the finals. Rudi had six assists in the tournament, and got his only goal in a 6-1 game against a Canadian team that was aroused to do well in the final, as a result of their loss to Austria. Although, disappointed with a silver medal, the German team had performed heroically in a tournament in which they were not expected to win a game.

GERMAN GAMES
Germany Defeated Great Britain 4-2
Germany Defeated Hungary 4-1
Germany Defeated Poland 3-1
Germany Defeated Switzerland 2-1
Germany Lost to Canada 6-1

Unlike today's hockey teams, most teams in those days were made up of from 7 to 10 players; consequently, in many cases a player would be on the ice for the entire 60 minutes. The players had to be in superb condition to have the stamina to withstand the gruelling skating up and down the ice, and to take crushing hits with almost no equipment to protect them. There were times when teams had to finish games with as few as three players due to injuries. Rudi was known as the iron man of German hockey, as he consistently logged over 50 minutes per game, and once played the entire 60 minutes for five straight games. This is a feat that few, if any, modern day players could even come close to duplicating.

The 1930 World Championships was a high point for German hockey, as not since that year have they been able to play in the championship game. Although Rudi's goal scoring was not up to par, his magnificent skating and stick handling made him a fan favourite. Additionally, his six assists were tops for the tournament. Always a superb playmaker, he made one particular pass that was talked about for years afterwards. Even fans who were not there would boast that they had seen Rudi rush down the right side of the rink, bounce the puck off the side boards, then as he skated around the defenseman, pick up the bouncing puck over the blue line, cross over to centre ice above the net in what appeared to be a clean breakaway and unselfishly make what was probably the first ever pass between his legs to the trailing Gustav Jaenecke, who effortlessly flipped the puck over the sprawling goalie into the upper right hand corner of the net. The fans applauded in total disbelief at what they witnessed.

The incredible skills exhibited by Jaenecke and Ball were particularly pleasing to the fans, but this tournament also solidified a friendship between these two players that would become legendary in the years leading up to and during World War II.

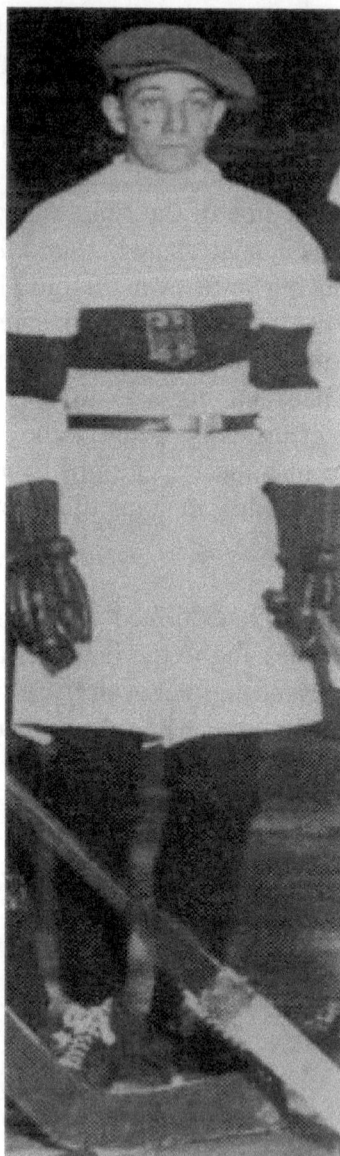

The Diminutive Rudi Ball in 1930 at Chamonix

The Rudi Ball Story

CHAPTER 3
THE GATHERING STORM

The 1931-1932 season was described by a French newspaper as the year of Rudi Ball. He seemed virtually unstoppable, and when it came time for Germany to select its Olympic team for the 1932 Olympics in Lake Placid, New York, Rudi was the uncontested number one selection, followed by his friend and line mate Gustav Jaenecke.

The III Winter Olympic Games in Lake Placid lost some of the normal lustre because of the severe economic conditions of the time caused by the Great Depression. However, the combination of Ball and Jaenecke electrified the fans with their scoring prowess. With Canada and the USA meeting in the Gold Medal game (won by Canada), Germany was matched against Poland for the Bronze Medal. Having narrowly defeated Poland (2-1) in their first game of the tournament, this game was highly anticipated, as Poland had used tough, hard-hitting play that seemed to slow down the fleet-footed Germans in the first meeting.

The Poles were not prepared to go quietly, as they used hard-checking to throw the Germans off their fleet-footed fast game that relied on pin-point passing and superior skating skills. Following a hard fought, check-filled, scoreless first period, Rudi started the second period with an amazing back-hand shot that went into the upper left-hand corner of the net, putting the Germans ahead 1-0. Two minutes into the third period, Poland pulled even with a shot from the point. Only two minutes later, Rudi took a pass mid-ice from Jaenecke, skated between two players, reversed direction, hit Jaenecke with a pass, skated to the right of the net and took a return pass from Jaenecke. Rudi slid the puck between the goalie's pads with ease, putting Germany up 2-1.

Germany's third goal was scored by Georg Strobl on a pass from Rudi. Near the end of the period, Rudi drove home another goal, becoming the first German player to record a hat trick in the Olympics, as Germany won the game 4-1. The bronze medal would be a highlight of German Olympic hockey for nearly fifty years.

Rudi Ball's 1932 Jersey

Much bigger than Ball, Jaenecke was a physically imposing compliment to Rudi's playmaking and skating skills. This combination accounted for 65% of all goals scored by the German National Team in 1932.

Later that spring, Germany lost only one of four games at the 1932 World Championships in Berlin, but because of the complicated rating system still finished out of the medals. Although the defence allowed just three goals, the offence seemed unable to match their play in the Olympics, and lost the final game of the tournament to Sweden 1-0.

The Rudi Ball Story

The years 1931-1932 had been extremely successful for German team, Berliner SC and Rudi, but, at the same time, Hitler was solidifying and sanctifying his political appeal and the people of Germany were unaware of what lay ahead for them in the gathering storm.

Gustav Jaenecke Moves Into Position for One of Rudi Ball's Precision Passes That Made the Two of Them so Deadly Every Time They Were on the Ice.

1932 German Olympic Team (Rudi – First From Left)

**Rare Photograph of Renowned Norwegian
Figure Skater, Sonja Henie
With Gustav Jaenecke at 1932 Olympics**

The Rudi Ball Story

Poster for the 1932 Lake Placid, New York (USA) Olympics

CHAPTER 4
CRUMBLING THE WALLS OF TYRANNY

When Rudi Ball crossed the blue line, his eyes gleamed like beacons shining from a light house. Goalies often said they felt like they were standing in the middle of a street and a car was headed for them at maximum speed. When goalies saw Rudi rev up his stride and hurl toward them like a cannonball, they often shook with fear. One goalie when asked to describe Rudi, used only one word, "terrifying."

As Swiss Defenseman Sprawls On The Ice In Disbelief, Rudi Ball, Scores A Goal After Skating Through Switzerland's Entire Team In A Dramatic End-To-End Rush. (This is the same goalie when asked to describe Rudi, simply said, "terrifying.")

As Rudi's reputation grew, someone else's reputation was also growing. Increasingly, Adolph Hitler was captivating the long-suffering German people with oratory that assured them that he and the Nazi party were the only answer to their misery that was caused by Jews and countries bent on ruining Germany.

After the Olympics, Rudi was hailed as an athletic hero in Germany, and the 1932-1933 season reunited him with his brothers Heinz and Gerhard on the Berliner SC team. That was not only a great year for Rudi, Heinz and Gustav Jaenecke, but was a season that saw Gerhard proclaimed the best goalie in Europe by many sports writers and fans, as he turned in sterling performances game after game.

**Cartoon That Appeared in Several Newspapers Depicting Gerhard Ball's Incredible Goaltending.
Respectful of His Brothers, Rudi Always
Praised Both Gerhard and Heinz for Their Abilities.**

How Hockey Saved A Jew From The Holocaust

Winning the German championship in 1933 with Berliner SC, Rudi was picked for the German team that would represent the country at the 1933 World Championships in Prague, Czechoslovakia. However, his brothers were left off the team and Germany's performance was disappointing. Yet, Rudi stood out once again with six goals in six games. His most important goal came on a breakaway that electrified the crowd in the last minute of the third period of a 1-1 tie with arch-rival Switzerland that assured Germany third place in European hockey.

1933 was also the year that would live in infamy as the President of Germany, Paul von Hindenburg, was forced by deteriorating economic conditions and political turmoil to appoint Adolph Hitler as Chancellor. This seemingly innocuous act would lead to Hitler almost immediately accumulating power and changing the nature of the Chancellor's job. After only two months in office, the Nazi's used the burning of the Reichstag building to pass the Enabling Act, which gave the Chancellor full legislative power for four years. This law allowed the Chancellor to introduce any law without consulting Parliament. By 1934, when von Hindenburg died, Hitler used the Enabling Act to merge the office of Chancellor and President, thereby creating a new office, Fuhrer. Hitler, as Fuhrer, became the dictator of Germany and unleashed a reign of inexorable cruelty.

As these political events unfolded, Rudi and his brothers received an offer to play for EHC St. Moritz in Switzerland for the 1933-34 season. Both Gerhard and Heinz had played abroad briefly in London during 1930 for the London Lions and won the British championship.

Rudi was a bit hesitant, but his brothers convinced him that this would be a great career move.

The St. Moritz offence revolved around Rudi, who was the star of the team. He averaged one goal per game, and the team had a successful season, which included a near victory over the Canadian team.

While Rudi and his brothers played in St. Moritz, dramatic events were taking place in Germany. Shortly after Hitler's appointment, the Nazis began a public policy of persecuting the Jews, communists, Gypsies (Roma) and homosexuals. They were particularly savage in their attacks on Jews. The government enacted a series of anti-Jewish laws, restricting the rights of German Jews to earn a living, have full-citizenship, to educate themselves or to serve in the civil service. It became government policy to require that all non-Jews had to boycott Jewish businesses. Jewish businesses were marked with the "Star of David," so that people knew that those places were off-limits to non-Jews. The result of these laws was the gradual exclusion of Jews from German political and social life. By 1935, these laws would revoke citizenship completely for Jews and forbid them from marrying non-Jewish Germans.

In April of 1933, the Nazi Sports Office implemented an "Aryan's Only" policy that excluded Jewish athletes from all sports clubs and they were not be allowed to compete against non-Jews. Despite these laws, Rudi was asked to play on the German national team in the 1934 World Championships in Milan, Italy. Although Rudi was concerned about what was happening to Jews in Germany, when he was asked to play, he enthusiastically accepted. Many years later, when asked by a Canadian journalist, Matthew Halton, why he agreed to play for Germany when it was obvious that Jews were being persecuted, he said, "I belong to the Jewish faith, but I am a German regardless of my faith."

Defeating Switzerland 2-1 in two overtimes at Milan, Italy, the German team was able to claim the European title once again; although they finished third behind Canada and the USA in the World Championships that year.

1934 World Championships

1. Canada, 2. USA, 3. Germany, 4. Switzerland,
5. Czechoslovakia, 6. Hungary, 7. Austria ,
8. Great Britain , 9. Italy, 10. Romania,
11. France, 12. Belgium

After the championships, all three Ball brothers were offered a contract to play for HC Milan Davoli Rosso Neri in the Italian Hockey League. They played there for the 1934-1935 (won Spengler Cup) and 1935-1936 seasons. Meanwhile, back in Germany, the Nazis were systematically making things more difficult for all who opposed them.

Rudi and his brothers played in Italy, but in the off-season, they lived in Berlin, so they could be close to their families. Life became increasingly difficult for them, as even their status as renowned athletes did not always keep them from persecution for being Jewish. (Jews were forced to wear a Star of David as identification starting in 1933 – see page 43).

Jews Were Forced to Wear a Star of David

In 1933, Hitler (Standing at the Lectern in the Middle) Addressed the Reichstag to Urge the Passage of Laws Denying Rights to the Jews and Other Groups (Homosexuals, Communists, Gypsies) Considered Enemies of the State.

**All Jewish Businesses Had to Be Painted With
The Star of David And/Or Have The Word Jew
Prominently Painted On
The Outside of The Businesses**

**Many Church Officials Were
Expected to Support the Nazis.**

The Nazis Used Propaganda Aimed at German Christians To Vilify Jews Based on Biblical Texts. Many Christian Ministers Supported Hitler's Policies, as They Blamed the Jews for the Death of Christ. (The words on the inscription at the bottom read: "When you see a cross, then think of the horrible murder of Jesus by the Jews.")

„Wenn ihr ein Kreuz seht, dann denkt an den grauenhaften Mord der Juden auf Golgatha..."

All School Text Books In Germany Had to Be Approved By the Nazi Party. Below Is a Sample of Anti-Semitism From a Book. Today, There are Still Countries that Use Textbooks for Propaganda, Promoting Certain Economic, Religious and Moral Specifics Defined By Those In Power.

As Two Boys Head To School, Jews Read a Sign That Says: "Jews not wanted here."

Sign Reads: "Residential Area – Entry Forbidden."

How Hockey Saved A Jew From The Holocaust

While anti-Semitism was growing in Germany, Rudi continued his stellar career, ever mindful of the growing dangers to him and his family. The years 1935 and 1936 were particularly brutal for German Jews. Below is an example of how Jews were isolated.

Hitler and his henchmen knew that by reaching the youth of Germany and indoctrinating them at an early age, they would have individuals who were convinced of the superiority of the Aryan race, and would be willing to die for the Fatherland. Each day, before the start of school, students were required to stand, give the Nazi salute, shout "Sieg Heil" and recite a pledge to support Germany in all her endeavours. In today's world, there are still many societies that use this type of indoctrination to instil ideas of superiority and obedience in young people. (Below is an illustration of school children being indoctrinated by pledging allegiance to the German nation and Adolph Hitler.)

In 1936, Rudi assumed that he would be left off the German Olympic team because of his Jewish heritage. Yet, he was to learn his team-mates, and particularly, Gustav Jaenecke, would give true meaning to what he once read in school, "strong-willed men united can crumble the walls of tyranny."

CHAPTER 5
STANDING TALL AGAINST THE WINDS OF TYRANNY

In order to understand the complexity of the situation that faced Rudi Ball in 1936, we must first go back to 1931, when the International Olympic Committee awarded both the winter and summer games to Germany. (The only time that both winter and summer games were awarded to the same country.) At the time, Hitler was not in power, and no one had any idea that the Nazis would take over. The winter games would be held in Garmisch Partenkirchen and the summer games in Berlin. Within a year, Hitler was in power, and with the consolidation of his power, a plethora of anti-Semitic laws (see previous chapter) became a part of German life. These laws even included a complete cultural purge of Jews from the fine arts, music, theatre, literature, the press, radio and film. By the end of 1933, these areas were declared by the Reich Chamber of Culture to be Judenrein. Soon the idea of Judenrein became a part of the sports establishment as well. It became accepted policy to not allow Jews to compete with or against Aryans.

Hitler was obsessed with the idea of Aryan superiority, and saw the Olympics as an opportunity to show the whole world German greatness and supremacy by winning as many medals as possible. Understanding the importance of propaganda, Hitler thought the games were a chance to make the world cower in fear of a physically superior race. For him, this was a means for gaining respectability among nations. Sports was much more than athletic contests. It was a way of reducing athletics to a battle between the rest of the world and Germany to prove which country was truly the most physically superior, and therefore morally, culturally and intellectually pre-eminent.

In the United States, some groups were opposed to sending a team to Germany, because of the exclusion of Jews. However, the Germans were quick to point out that the Americans had for years allowed discrimination against its Black citizens, especially in the south, where Blacks were required to use separate public facilities from Whites. Particular reference was made to laws allowing segregation in public schools and housing. The head of the German Olympic Committee also pointed out that Blacks were not allowed to play in major league baseball at the time. Additionally, Joseph Goebbles asked the Americans to explain why they had confiscated Indian land and locked Native Americans up in reservations to segregate them from the rest of society. He said the Americans were hypocritical for attacking others for doing what they had done in their own country. This same argument was used by the International Olympic Committee when the USA petitioned for the games to be moved to another location.

The head of the U.S. Olympic Committee was Avery Brundage, who had once proposed that women be excluded from the games. He insisted that it would be inappropriate for the USA to boycott the Olympics, as it might lead to a boycott by Germany in the future. Known as a Nazi sympathizer, Brundage had attended a large pro-Nazi rally in Madison Square Garden, where he was a featured speaker. Additionally, his construction firm was awarded a contract to build the German embassy in Washington DC.

How Hockey Saved A Jew From The Holocaust

This was the beginning of the modern Olympics that became more of a business venture than an athletic endeavour. Many U.S. companies began to see the Olympic movement as a way to advertise their products, and they did not want to let Nazism interfere with corporations making money from the biggest sporting event in the world. Additionally, newspapers and radio stations covered the games, so a boycott would have adverse effects on their advertising revenue. All these entities lobbied the U.S. government to make sure there was no boycott.

Avery Brundage decried all the furor over Jews being excluded from the team by saying the fact that no Jews have been named so far to compete for Germany doesn't mean that they have been discriminated against on that score ." He was also rumoured to indicate in private that maybe there were no Jews in Germany athletically talented enough to make the team. As late as 1971, he was still insisting that the German games of 1936 were the best in Olympic history.

**German Newspapers Ran This Picture Showing
White People In the USA Laughing at
The Lynching of Two Blacks**

**The Below Photo Appeared In
Several German Newspapers That Criticized
The USA For Wanting to Boycott
The German Olympics Because of Discrimination
Against The Jews,
When America Was Discriminating Against Blacks**

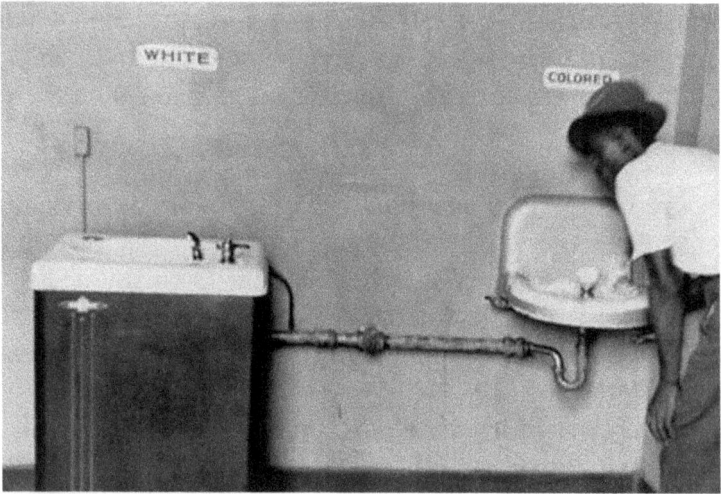

Canada was considering a boycott, but after pressure from the USA and Great Britain (both countries thought they had hockey teams capable of finally beating the Canadian team which had never lost an Olympic hockey game), Canada acquiesced, and decided to attend. The British would actually wind-up defeating the Canadians 2-1 for the Gold Medal, as 10 of their 12 players had lived in Canada most of their lives and played hockey there. The game also featured a large fight that almost led to both teams being disqualified. This is still considered one of the greatest upsets in Olympic history, as Canada had won four straight gold medals and 20 straight games before losing to the British team.

How Hockey Saved A Jew From The Holocaust

Seeing the turmoil in Germany, Rudi, while visiting France in 1935, refused to return home. Meanwhile, Rudi's family was suffering persecution. Living in exile Rudi knew there was no chance for him to play on the German Olympic team. When the Minister of German Sport named the team, Rudi was indeed left off. However, Gustav Jaenecke, who was the first selection for the team, made it plain that he would not be participating if Rudi was not included. The rest of the team backed Jaenecke, and, for the first time, a group of individuals stood up to Hitler's policies of Judenrein. If Germany was to have a credible team, some accommodations would have to be made with these young men who were refusing to allow the Nazi prejudice to be applied to their team-mate.

When word of what had occurred got back to the Ministry of Sport, threats were made against Jaenecke and his team-mates. However, the team was unified in its support of Rudi Ball. Eventually, Hitler, himself, got involved and realized that if word got out about the team refusing to play without their Jewish star; it would reflect unfavourably on the entire Nazi effort to make the games a display of German unity and might. For that reason, he instructed the Ministry of Sport to contact Rudi in France and ask him to play.

Aware of how his team-mates had stood by him, Rudi felt an obligation to play. However, he also saw it as an opportunity to get his entire family out of Germany, so they could avoid the coming calamity. Before agreeing to play, he insisted that his family be allowed to leave Germany. Within four weeks, the entire Ball family, with the exception of Rudi, had been given permission to immigrate to South Africa. Years later, the family would realize that had it not been for Rudi's hockey playing ability, they would have all likely died in a concentration-camp.

Not only did Rudi's team-mates stand-up to the Nazis and insist that he be included on the team, they unanimously elected him captain; thereby, infuriating the Nazi hierarchy even more. When told of the decision to make him captain, Hitler is reported to have said, "if all Germans were like these hockey players, I would have never been made Chancellor."

For the first time in years, Hitler was being challenged, but he felt he could do nothing about it, because he was using the games as propaganda tool to promote the superiority of the Nazis. There were only three ways around the dilemma. He could replace the team and lose, refuse to accede to the players wishes and lose, or give in to their demands and maybe win. His back was against the wall and he knew it. He chose to give in to the team and hopefully win at least a bronze medal for the German nation.

Resigned to having to accept a Jew on the German Olympic squad, Hitler was not particularly pleased, but he had finally come upon a group of individuals who were determined to stand up against his tyranny. Had the rest of Germany been as strong-willed as these brave young men, the history of German, the world and six million Jews would have been much different.

Now that Rudi's family was safe, he started preparing to do all he could to win a medal for the German team, in spite of his great disdain for Adolph Hitler and all he stood for in a world that was just beginning to comprehend the evil of the Nazi menace that was engulfing Germany and would soon spread like an ancient plague throughout Europe. In spite of the dangers of staying in Germany, Rudi was a man of his word, and he would live up to his commitment to represent Germany in the 1936 Olympics. He owed it to his team-mates, and particularly to Gustav Jaenecke, who had stood tall against the winds of tyranny.

The German Olympic Logo For The 1936 Games

CHAPTER 6
TODAY IS OUR DAY, NOT YOURS

For Hitler and the Nazis, the games were to be a display of Aryan superiority. Rudi found it ironic that he, a non-Aryan, had been selected to promulgate this absurd idea. Yet, he had made an agreement, and he did consider himself a loyal German; consequently, although he disagreed with the Nazis, he was determined to try as hard as he could to see that Germany won a medal in hockey. He also thought, as a Jew, he was proving that Hitler's idea of racial superiority had no basis in fact. Rudi felt that he and his team-mates could show that all Germans, regardless of their ethnicity, could work together toward a common goal. Unfortunately, the Nazis were not interested in listening to the opinions of anyone who opposed their ideas of racial purity. However, the German hockey team was united in defying Hitler and the Nazis' ideas of Aryan superiority. Standing up for Rudi, they were among the very few whose resistance was tolerated by Hitler.

Hitler looked on the games in Garmisch-Partenkirchen as an opportunity to showcase Aryan supremacy and German glory. He felt the winter games were nothing more than a prelude to the summer games, which would give him an even greater chance to exhibit the splendour of Berlin to the entire world. The winter games would have only one star – Adolph Hitler. The man who had rebuilt Germany in the face of global depression, lifted the country from the ashes of war and turned it into a military power had great hopes riding on the hockey team, and he knew that the success of the team was riding on two men, Rudi Ball and Gustav Jaenecke. The odds were against them winning a medal at all, but with a team unified and devoted to one another, there was always a chance that impossible odds could be overcome. The team was determined and determination can often conquer insurmountable barriers. After all, hadn't Hitler, himself, overcome insurmountable odds?

Even though the team did not share Hitler's views, they were still proud Germans, and the players all vowed to represent Germany in the best fashion possible.

Hitler At the Opening Ceremonies

For years, the German state had secretly funded the hockey program. Ice hockey was the most popular team sport at the winter games, and was, therefore, the greatest prize. Yet, for the Germans to win, they had to field a team capable of beating the greatest hockey team in the world, the Canadians. Hitler felt that the task was almost impossible, but that under the leadership of Rudi Ball and Gustav Jaenecke, there was a good chance that they could pull off the first ever upset of the Canadian Olympic hockey team which had won 4 straight gold medals and never lost in the Olympic games. The games themselves were to be a coming-out party for Hitler that would bring great glory to the Third Reich. And there could be no greater glory than defeating the Canadians.

For the Nazis, winning was about more than national pride; it was about racial pride. Yet, this racial pride had been compromised by a team that refused to play without the inclusion of Germany's foremost hockey player, who just happened to be Jewish.

The Nazis saw sport as a way to strengthen the German character, imbuing it with the fighting spirit and steadfast camaraderie necessary to make Germany the ruler of the world. By developing sport to its highest form, Nazis believed that Aryan youth could be strengthened, and in the end, better prepared for war. Yet, the hockey team seemed to care nothing about the idea of racial superiority. Their only concern was to play as well as possible, and maybe be able to finally beat the Canadians. For that reason, they did not care about the Nazi racial views. They simply wanted to put out the best team possible, so when the war on the ice was over, they could stand victorious for their country, not for some idiotic idea of racial superiority, but for the Germany they all loved.

Too often, in international sporting events between the two world wars, competition took on the air of defending a nation's honor. Cultural differences, political ideologies and blind patriotism supplanted sportsmanship. Pride and emotion often replaced reason. Yet, ice hockey had always been played as a war-on-ice. Unlike other sports, it demanded a devotion to organized mayhem on the part of participants. The sheer energy level required made it singularly unique among all sports. The fact that players carried around the equivalent of a weapon (sticks) in their hands required a discipline not expected in other sports. Even the few times that international competition had led to fisticuffs, the altercations seemed to never dampen the mutual respect hockey players had for each other. When the battle was over, the participants lined up, shook hands and got ready for the next war-on-ice. Fortunately, Rudi and his team-mates had the character to realize that the integrity of the game was more important than Nazi ideology that emphasized racial superiority.

Controversy arose right from the start of the games, as the opening ceremonies were a display of intense and fanatical Nazi propaganda with an exhibition of ice dancers and military personnel that emphasized the Aryan nature of Hitler's Germany, as well as the superior character of German culture. The opening ceremonies include a march of all the athletes past the reviewing stand where they salute the officials and dip their flags in respect. Ironically, the official Olympic salute at this time was very similar to the Nazi salute. Several teams refused to make the salute and only turned their heads right toward the reviewing stand.

The other major controversy was over the Great Britain hockey team of 12 players, which included 10 Canadians who had been born in Britain and had dual citizenship. The International Olympic Committee refused to bar them from playing, in spite of protests from Canada and several other countries.

Germany's first game was against the USA. After Canada, the USA was considered the best team. However, playing superb defence, the German team managed to hold the USA scoreless for two periods. Rudi was skating splendidly, and made several pin-point passes that almost led to goals by Gustav Jaenecke. Third period German penalties gave the USA a two-man advantage, and they managed to score a goal. The 1-0 loss was particularly heartbreaking for Rudi and his team-mates, because they had played so well against a team that was supposed to beat them handily.

Germany's next game was against a feisty Italian team that was known for extremely rough play. However, the superior skating abilities of the Germans kept the Italians off-balance most of the game. Although not scoring any goals, Rudi set up scores by his team-mates in a thrilling 3-0 victory.

The Feisty Italian Team

The Rudi Ball Story

How Hockey Saved A Jew From The Holocaust

Garmisch Partenkirchen Stadium
Where The Opening Ceremonies Took Place

The most intense rivalry was between Germany and Switzerland. Although Hitler was more concerned with displaying Aryan superiority, the real German hockey fans enjoyed the contests between these two rivals, because they were neighbouring countries, and most Swiss people spoke German. For many years they had engaged in titanic struggles on the ice, and this game was the one Germans really wanted to see. Over 10,000 fans turned out, which, at the time, was the largest crowd to ever see an Olympic hockey game. Rudi Ball and company would not disappoint the fans. In fact, this game would often be described as one of Rudi's finest hours; although he only scored one goal and had one assist. The goal and assist total was immaterial to the role he played as leader of the team.

Described by one journalist as being similar to a painter,

How Hockey Saved A Jew From The Holocaust

Rudi's canvas was the ice, skates his palette and the stick his brush. It was as if he was painting a masterpiece with ever stride up the ice.Rudi painted a lovely picture on ice that day, painting what he felt about hockey. The ice was his refuge from the storms of Hitler's tyranny. The ice was his shelter from the tempest of deceit practiced by those who wanted to enslave all humanity to the evils of racism. The ice was the blanket that warmed him from the cold of an evil perpetrated by those who pointed the finger of condemnation. It was the pillow upon which he could rest his hopes and shed his tears of anguish. The ice was his heaven, more beautiful than anything he had ever seen in his 25 years.

This was the day described by a fan as the most magnificent display ever witnessed of a man's love for a game. Rudi Ball represented the pure essence of hockey this day. Setting up Gustav Jaenecke for the first goal, Rudi picked up the puck in his defensive end at the blue line. Avoiding a check with a nifty move, he skated tight against the boards as he raced up ice, moved to the centre of the rink with a long, smooth stride and maneuvered through two players at the opponent's blue line. The goalie moved out of goal, expecting a booming shot from Rudi. Rudi skated in on the goalie, but dropped the puck behind him for Jaenecke, who picked it up and drove it home over the prone goalie who had been expecting a shot from Rudi. This unselfish play brought 10,000 fans, both German and Swiss, to their feet, applauding wildly for a man who truly knew the meaning of the word team. Personal glory never entered into Rudi's thoughts. His only thought was to see that his team won the game. As the players on his team swarmed around him, the fans continued their wild applause. On the ice, even the Swiss team stood in awe, shaking their heads in disbelief at what they had witnessed. Adolph Hitler, in the stands to support Aryan superiority, stood with his head bowed, because the team was swarming around Rudi, and the German fans were applauding for a Jew.

As great as that play was, Rudi was not finished. Late in the third period, with the weather turning colder, Rudi's smooth, methodical strides seemed to make him glisten in the fading sun like silver thread on black cloth. The Swiss fans were cheering their team on to score the tying goal. It seemed they would score, when a Swiss player was left alone at centre ice and took a pass from a defenseman. As he headed up ice, there was no one near him, but like a streak of lightning in a raging summer thunder storm, Rudi dipped his head and moved up the ice like a cannonball. At the blue line, the Swiss player moved to his right and out of nowhere, came Rudi sliding across the ice with his stick extended as far as he could reach. The tip of his blade hooked under the Swiss players stick, lifting it and the puck flittered harmlessly into the corner. Rudi got to his feet in full stride, going to the corner to pick up the puck. He immediately skated behind the net. Looking up ice, he skated with intensity to his right, moving up ice rapidly. Gliding by the right boards, the fans were on their feet, applauding his incredible defensive play. As a Swiss player lowered his shoulder and lined him up for a check, Rudi literally jumped off the ice, leaving nothing but the boards for the player to ram into head first. He jumped so high that it seemed he was airborne. He made a reverse move while in the air, completely confounding a defensemen at the blue line. Coming down on his right skate, he skated along the blue line until he was at centre ice. Although he had not scored, the fans were all on their feet now, applauding the magnificent display of skating prowess. Making a sharp turn to the left, he drew the remaining defenseman toward the left boards. Then when he had the defenseman committed, he leaned to his right on one skate, pushing the puck between the defenseman's legs on his backhand. Picking the puck up with a deft move using the tip of his stick blade, the defenseman could only look in bewilderment as Rudi moved toward the goal. While the goalie moved out of his net to cut down the angle, Rudi pivoted on his right skate, lifting the puck up on the blade of his stick and easily flipped it over the left shoulder of the goalie. It dropped to the ice just behind the goal line, and the fans erupted in unison to applaud one of the most remarkable exhibitions of goal scoring in Olympic history. Rudi Ball was mobbed by his team-mates, and all the Swiss team could do was marvel at what Rudi had done. . The 2-0 victory over their rivals was to be the highlight of the Olympics for the German team, as the next game would lead to a tragic end of the Olympics for Rudi.

On 11 February 1936, Rudi woke up around 4:00 AM in anticipation of that day's game against Hungary. A victory against the Hungarians would assure them a shot at the Canadian led Great Britain team and maybe a gold medal. At the very least, a silver medal was a real possibility. For some reason, Rudi felt apprehensive. At the early morning skate, he and Gustav Jaenecke seemed to be slightly off with their pin-point passing that was their usual hallmark. Rudi was aware that all of Germany, and especially Adolph Hitler, was anxiously awaiting today's game. Their victory over archrival Switzerland had swelled all Germans with pride, but now the hopes of a nation for a Gold Medal rested on the shoulders of 10 young men who had stood against the evils of oppression and despotism at a time when other Germans refused to stand up to the tyranny that was gripping the nation.

Knowing the importance of the contest, Rudi called the team together for a meeting before the game. He turned to his fellow players and said, "All of you made it possible for me to be here. I am not playing for Germany, I am playing for you. I am indebted to you, and I shall never be able to repay you for your kindness and devotion. No man has ever been more humbled than I am today. I truly have learned the meaning of friendship thanks to all of you. I am privileged to share this moment with you, and I will forever honor and respect your devotion, not just to me, but to the sanctity of all that is good in the hearts of men who stand up for what is right and just."

Together, they all rose, stood in silence and waited for their captain to lead them onto the ice. As they skated onto the rink, 10,000 fans stood to cheer a team that was more than just a group of hockey players. These men were bold Knights wearing the armor of modern hockey warriors who were there to do battle on ice, not for the glory of Adolph Hitler and his asinine ideas of racial superiority, but for the honor and dignity of men bound by their devotion to one another. Their bearing and manner, as they glided gracefully toward their bench seemed almost surreal, while the sun peeped through the overcast sky, shining its light directly on the German team as they settled into their places on the bench.

Hungary, in its earlier games had destroyed Belgium

11-2 and humiliated a highly rated French team. They had even held off a physically superior Czech team until the final minutes when penalties did them in and gave the Czechs a narrow victory. Only Germany stood in the way of a Hungarian march into the finals and Olympic glory.

As Adolph Hitler arrived in the filled-to-capacity stadium the fans cheered wildly. Rudi looked up to the Fuhrer's box, and along with his team-mates turned his head back toward the ice. As the "Sieg Heils" rumbled and shook the stadium, each German player stood staring straight ahead. They were one. This was the true meaning of a team. It was as if each player was saying, "today is our day, not yours."

Hitler at the Germany – Hungary Game

How Hockey Saved A Jew From The Holocaust

**Germany-Hungary Game
Garmisch-Partenkirchen Stadium**

CHAPTER 7
THERE IS BLOOD ON THE BATTLEFIELD

The course of human events sometimes seems beyond the ability of mere mortals to comprehend. Why things happened the day of the Germany-Hungary game the way they did defies explanation in many ways. It was to be one of Rudi's greatest triumphs, but it would end in disaster, as so many triumphs do. Just when things seem to be going well, fate can often intervene to bring us all to the reality that we sometimes are simply victims of chance.

Rudi and his team-mates were playing a Hungarian team that, like the Germans, was motivated to achieve something they had never imagined possible a few months before. Both teams were on the brink of doing something they had never been able to accomplish in the Olympics. Germany had won a medal before, but in this Olympics, both teams had an opportunity at gold. This was a game that would see both teams ask for no quarter and give no quarter. This was a war.

These men all lived by a special code of mutual respect, only understood by those who have laced up skates, grabbed sticks and skated onto a field of honor called a hockey rink. It is within the confines of this field of battle that ice-warriors of mayhem match skills, determination and desire to see who emerges victorious. Yet, even those who are vanquished must not bow their heads in shame, because the ice rink is a field of honor that signifies human effort and endeavour of the highest form. Losers are not really losers, as long as they know they have given their all to the effort. This day, one team would skate off a winner on the scoreboard, but neither team was defeated, because every man showed the utmost in bravery, honor, dedication and skill.

Looking at his team-mates as they lined-up for the face-off, this was the day Rudi Ball genuinely understood the meaning of love. Love was not a feeling. It was an activity and an investment in those to whom you felt a kinship. This game was his opportunity to show love for his team-mates, who had risked their own well-being for his benefit. This would be an epic battle and Rudi would be the general.

When the whistle blew and the puck was dropped, German players hit the deck, as the Hungarians unloaded their fury with brutal body checks. With seconds left in the first period, Rudi, streaking up rink, was slammed by two Hungarians, his head banging onto the ice. There was blood and pain in his forehead, but, like a jack-in-the-box at the end of the tune, he popped up in full stride to furiously move into the Hungarian zone and retrieve the puck. Moving to his right as the goalie hunched in anticipation of a shot, Rudi spotted Jaenecke flying down the right wing. Leveled with a mighty check from the defenseman, Rudi heard a loud pop in his shoulder as it hit the ice. Yet, as he sprawled on the ice in pain, his stick somehow managed to find the puck and he flicked it perfectly onto Jaenecke's stick blade. The goalie, in disbelief, watched helplessly as Jaenecke drove the puck home into the upper right hand corner of the net. Cheers thundered from the crowd, but died down as Jaenecke and his team-mates bent over Rudi, who was still sprawled on the ice in pain. Somehow, Rudi managed to get to his feet. The pain was excruciating, but Rudi insisted he was fine.

Not being able to move his left shoulder, the coach insisted he sit for awhile. Protesting the decision, Rudi was adamant that he was fine. Still, he sat, and sat, and sat............

In the second period, with Rudi still on the bench, Hungary tied the score 1-1 on a power play goal. When Germany came out for the third period, the fans were despondent over the turn of events that had seen great promise deteriorate into despair. Rudi had not returned to the bench and Hungary was continuing to press hard, almost scoring several times, as Germany seemed to just be hanging on in desperation with only one minute left to play. Then, a stoppage of play occurred, and from behind the bench, a lone figure, with his left shoulder slightly dipping from intense pain, strode up to the boards, put his right hand on the ledge and hopped onto the ice. A roar went up from the crowd that was so loud it seemed to rattle off the mountains in the distance, and the stadium literally shook from the vibrations of pounding feet that rocked the countryside, as shouts of "Rudi, Rudi" reverberated throughout the quaint village like a bomb exploding on a quiet, distant land lost in time. Skating to his right wing position as the linesmen prepared for the face-off, Rudi returned to the battle. Scarred, torn, wracked with pain, somewhat bowed, but not humbled, Rudi was back on the battlefield. Determination, drive and desire was etched not only on his face, but you could see his resolve in the very way he leaned forward with his stick on the ice.

Rudi's deeply gashed forehead continued to bleed, dripping bright red droplets onto the battlefield. As the puck was dropped in the circle to the right of the German goalie, Rudi moved inside his opponent, picked up the skittering puck and slid it gracefully through the chaos, with long, smooth, steady strides. Crossing his own blue line, he deftly moved toward centre ice, flakes flying from the intensity of his masterful moves with skates that seemed as sharp as razor blades. He appeared to blur in the dash up ice as he cut back to his left, literally leaving the Hungarian player to glare in amazement as Rudi rushed by him like a hurricane hitting shore at full force. As he hit the Hungarian blue line, one defensemen moved toward Rudi while the other one slid quickly backward to position himself to the left of the goalie. Eyes red like a raging fire, Rudi gritted his teeth as the defensemen crushed him with a devastating check. The hit was high, hard, and ground deep into Rudi's injured left shoulder. Hearing another sickening pop, Rudi's body seemed to take flight as he hurdled through the air feet pointing skyward. Doing a complete summersault, remarkably, Rudi landed on his skates in full stride and was able to pick up the puck which had wobbled between the defenseman's legs. The other defenseman now moved toward Rudi, stick extended like a menacing weapon ready to carve up an opponent. With a pain wrecked body, Rudi absorbed a blow to his mid-chest, as the defenseman purposefully forced the stick between Rudi's legs, lifting him up onto the stick. Rudi was able to stay on his skates and keep his stick on the puck as the defenseman's right skate blade rose up and cut deep into Rudi's left thigh. Meanwhile, the goalie had moved to hug the right goal post, cutting off Rudi's best chance to score. Undeterred, Rudi pivoted on his right skate and with incredible artistry used the tip of his blade to ease the puck around the goalie's outstretched glove-hand and slam it into the back of the net. Pandemonium broke out in the stands, as even Hitler, the great hater of Jews, could not help but get to his feet and applaud with enthusiasm at what was indeed a marvel on ice.

Blood poring from a deep gash on his back left thigh, Rudi was hoisted up by two team-mates and escorted to the bench. Even one of the Hungarian players came up to Rudi and offered his congratulations. The few seconds left were played; after which, Rudi struggled to his feet and stood proud with his team-mates to bask in the glory of a moment that would live forever in the hearts of those who were there. They stood victorious with pride and dignity, because they had done more than win a game. They had stood together against a tyrant, when others were bowing in supplication to a man who would lead an entire nation to ruin. The heroics of Rudi Ball and the blood he left on the ice that day, motivated Wayne Frye in 1990 to immortalize the moment in a poem.

Blood on the Battlefield – The Rudi Ball Rush

There is blood on the battlefield.
The warrior's wounds have all healed.
But that glorious moment in Rudi Ball's mind is sealed.
There is blood on the battlefield.

The furious five headed down the rink.
Led by helmet-less Rudi Ball with a blood-stained glove.
The powerful German team was on the brink.
But this was more than a game; it was about love.

Suddenly, Rudi's blade edges seemed to ignite.
A burly defenseman tries to put him on the deck.
But Rudi avoids the check as he seems to take flight,

How Hockey Saved A Jew From The Holocaust

Blood streaming down his cheek, dropping on his neck.

Rudi, weaving and bobbing on a breakaway run,
The goalie standing defiant in his place.
Rudi thinks nobody will be standing when he is done,
As a smile creeps across his blood-stained face.

Loud roars rumble and thunder from the crowd.
Rudi pushes the puck gracefully, as he gets in his groove.
Regardless of the outcome his head will not be bowed.
He and his team-mates bravery leaves nothing to prove.

Another defensemen falls as Rudi cuts to his right.
He is now nothing but a blur across the ice.
Only seconds remain in his magnificent flight.
For victory he will make the supreme sacrifice.

The goalie makes his stand, not willing to concede.
Rudi's blades cut through the ice like a knife.
A goal, a goal, what else in life does he need,
As he puts behind him all the pain and strife.

Heading to the goal cage, he soars through the air.
Dancing around the last line of defence,
An opponent's errant blade slices his thigh bone bare.
Dismay quivers through the crowd caught in the suspense.

It is pride that drives Rudi toward the goal,
As he gently slides the puck into the net.
Bloodied and victorious, he is at peace in his soul.
This was a goal the evil tyrant would never forget.

Applauding a Jew, Hitler could not believe what he saw.
But Rudi's goal was neither for country or ruler supreme.

The Rudi Ball Story   71

How Hockey Saved A Jew From The Holocaust

He and his team-mates were above Hitler's law.
His goal was for his colleagues and an equalitarian dream.

There is blood on the battlefield.
The warrior's wounds have all healed.
But that glorious moment in Rudi Ball's mind is sealed.
There is blood on the battlefield.

**The Team That Stood-Up to Hitler
(Gustav Jaenecke, First From Left
Rudi is Fourth From the Left)**

The Rudi Ball Story

THE FOLLOWING PAGES HAVE

PHOTOS RELATING TO

THE PROPOSED BOYCOTT

AND

FROM

THE

1936

WINTER

OLYMPIC

GAMES

IN

GARMISCH-PARTENKIRCHEN,

GERMANY

****

An English reporter who had traveled to Garmisch-Partenkirchen. In the fall of 1935 and photographed the Partenkirchen Ski Club's clubhouse, where a sign reading "No Jews Allowed Here!" was posted on the wall. The image circled the globe and caused an outrage, especially in the USA, where a boycott was proposed. German newspapers responded with photographs like the ones on pages 51 and 52. The Berlin papers ran the photos on 77 and 78, accusing the USA of hypocrisy for ridiculing German discrimination when African-Americans were discriminated against in the USA. This caused Germany to go before the International Olympic Committee to ask why they allowed the summer games of 1932 in Los Angeles when the USA discriminated against African-Americans. The USA, fearing pressure from international organizations to end their own discriminatory policies decided it would be best not to pursue a boycott.

The Rudi Ball Story

The below photo taken at a Greensboro, North Carolina bus station appeared in many German newspapers as an illustration of the prejudice that existed against African-Americans in the USA.

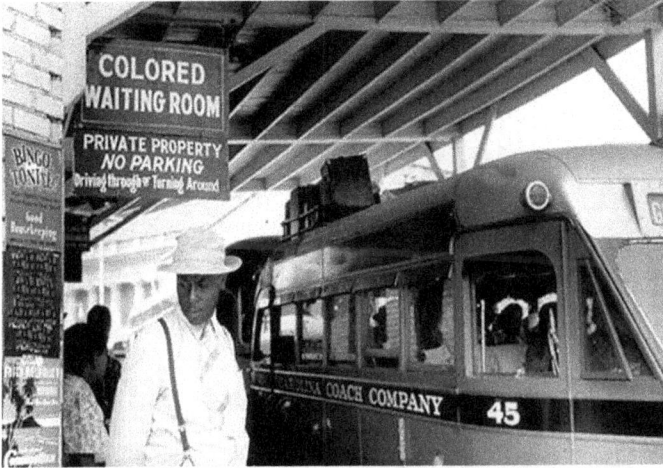

The below picture from Alabama was used by the German newspapers to illustrate that although signs in the USA might not say "Coloured People Not Allowed," there was an implication that they were not, as evidenced by the dress shop door sign below reading "White Ladies Only."

Hitler arrives in Garmisch-Partenkirchen to the wild cheers of the people. Bavarian resort Garmisch-Partenkirchen applied to host the 2018 Winter Olympics, which it last hosted in 1936. Locals still have fond memories of the games, but they have little interest in dealing with the idyllic Alpine town's uncomfortable past when Hitler used the Olympics as a showcase for his ideas of Aryan race superiority.

Willy Bogner of Germany swears the Olympic Oath during the opening ceremony of the 1936 Winter Olympic Games in Garmisch-Partenkirchen.

How Hockey Saved A Jew From The Holocaust

The German skier Christl Cranz was one of the stars of the 1936 Winter Olympics. Seen below on his way to winning the gold medal in the downhill, he was one of the many German athletes who feared what the Nazis reaction would be if they did not perform up to the expectations.

There was wide-spread concern and fear among the German athletes as a result of the pressure put on them by Hitler. Many of them, no doubt, did not perform as well as expected, as a result of this intimidation from Hitler who wanted to show entire world the superiority of the Aryan race.

The hockey team had already proved that they were not afraid to stand up to Hitler. Although they knew what could happen to them if they defied Hitler, they were united in their belief that they had to stand up for the right of their teammate to play. This bold stand was one of the few times any group of people openly defied the will of Adolph Hitler.

How Hockey Saved A Jew From The Holocaust

One of the greatest speed skaters of his time, Norwegian Ivar Ballangrud, won four world titles and four European titles. He competed in three Olympics, earning seven medals. The Norwegian athlete clinched three gold medals, in the 500 metres, the 5,000 metres and the 10,000 metres. He also won a silver medal in the 1,500 metres. Proclaimed the greatest speed skater of his time, when watching Rudi Ball in the game against Hungary at the 1936 Olympics, he said, "that man is the most remarkable skater I have ever seen."

Norwegian Ivan Ballangrud skating in 5000 metres.

The Rudi Ball Story

How Hockey Saved A Jew From The Holocaust

Hungary- Germany Game

Rudi Ball

EPILOGUE
IT SAVED ME FROM THE HOLOCAUST

Unfortunately, Rudi could not play the last two games because of his injuries. With a broken shoulder, a lacerated leg and a huge gash across his forehead, all Rudi could do was cheer on the team from the sidelines. Yet, the team almost pulled off a stunning upset of the Canadian laden British team that would win the gold medal, ending up with a 1-1 tie. However, they had to beat Canada in order to qualify for a medal. The Canadian team was already seething with anger when their protests about Canadians being on the British team had been disregarded. Realizing the British were going to win the gold medal, they decided to take their fury out on the hapless German team that was without their star player and, now, Gustav Jaenecke was also ailing. In front of a crowd that included Propaganda Minister, Joseph Goebbels and 10,000 German fans, Canada treated the opposition to a lesson in the art of body-checking and cheerfully proceeded to thump the injury-plagued German team nearly senseless. Although the checks were legal, the German fans howled in outrage as the Canadians won 6-2.

Disappointed, but still proud of their accomplishments, these players would forever remember their dedication to one another, and Rudi would never forget how they had made it possible for his family to get out of Germany and avoid the Holocaust.

While Rudi and his team-mates were doing all they could to bring victory to Germany, often, outside the rink there would be a parade of youths carrying swastikas and shouting, "The Jews must be destroyed." Most of them had no idea that the hero of the games was a 25 year old Jew named Rudi Ball. A recognizable figure throughout Germany, few people realized that the greatest hockey player in the nation was a Jew.

Following the Olympics, Rudi stayed in Germany and played for Berliner SC. In 1937, he led them to the German championship against SC Riessersee. The first game ended in dramatic 1-1 tie, with Rudi scoring the only Berliner goal with 3 seconds to play. After three scoreless overtime periods, the game was called. When resumed a few days later, Rudi scored a goal early in the game to seal the victory.

Throughout the war years (1939-1945), Rudi continued to play with Berliner SC, as Hitler insisted that the people needed diversions from the war, and sports offered the people a chance to get their minds off all the deprivation. Even though Jews were being rounded up and sent to concentration camps, no one seemed concerned that Rudi was Jewish.

Unable to get out of Germany, Rudi lived in fear that one day, the authorities would come to pick him up. Yet, since he was a revered and beloved hockey player, the Nazis seemed content to ignore him. In 1944, the devastation of Germany was almost complete and most of the ice rinks had been destroyed. Waiting for the end of the war, Rudi barely survived, but thanks to friends like Gustav Jaenecke, there was always food on the table.

In May of 1945, much to the relief of Rudi, Berlin fell to the Allied armies. At the age of 35, Rudi had no profession, other than hockey. His entire family had left Germany, and as he sat alone in his apartment, there was a knock on the door. He opened it to find his brother Gerhard standing in the doorway. Smiling, Gerhard said, "Hey, brother, want to play some hockey?" And play hockey they did, as both players made a valiant comeback for SG Eichamp Berlin, where they played until 1948.

Rudi looked like the old days with his sharp skating and prodigious stick handling in the shortened season of 1946, averaging an incredible 3 goals a game. Meanwhile, his 43 year old brother was the premiere goalie in Germany. Although not winning the title, they did play in the German championships in 1946 and 1947.

Then in 1948, encouraged by his brother Heinz, Rudi moved to South Africa. He settled in Johannesburg, where he intended to go into business, but South Africa was filled with Dutch and German immigrants who loved hockey, so the only hockey league in Africa was formed, and Rudi simply could not leave the sport that had given him so much. He played for the Johannesburg Tigers in 1949-1950, averaging a goal a game. Slowing down at the age of 41, he played defence for the Johannesburg Wolves in the 1950-1951 season, again averaging a goal a game with limited playing time.

At the end of the 1951 season, 41 year old Rudi felt it was time to hang up his skates for good, but in 1952 he was lured out of retirement to play in an all-star game that pitted South African players against an incredibly talented all-star European team. Rudi's team won 10-4, with Rudi netting 4 goals himself, all in his usual dramatic fashion. After scoring over 500 goals in his career, the most feared

European player of his day skated off the ice for the last time.

Rudi became a respected and successful businessman in South Africa until his death in 1975. His good friend, Gustav Jaenecke, upon hearing of his death said, "Rudi was more than a great hockey player. He was a great person. That is the best epitaph a man can have."

Rudi was posthumously inducted into the International Ice Hockey Hall of Fame in 2004, when few people were still alive to remember his exploits in Europe as the most intimidating, determined and fearless player of his time. One attendee said, "Almost no one at the induction ceremony knew who Rudi Ball was. It is unfortunate that his exploits have been lost in the sands of time, because he was truly the very best of his generation of hockey players. His story is about more than hockey. It is about the power of a team to stand up to evil, and to rise above the pettiness that is so much a part of sports today."

In 1970, when interviewing Rudi, a journalist said, "you are a forgotten man in hockey. Don't you feel that hockey owes you more recognition than you have received?"

Rudi, without hesitation replied, "hockey owes me nothing. I am the one who owes hockey. It saved me and my family from the Holocaust."

STATISICAL INFORMATION FOR RUDI BALL

Born: March 27, 1910 in Berlin, Germany

Died: September 1975 in Johannesburg, South Africa

Shoots: Right

Height: 5' 4" (163 cm) **Weight:** 140 lbs. (63 kg)

Skates: Size 6 (36)

Clubs:
SC Brandenburg Berlin (1927-1928)
Berliner SC (1928-1933, 1936-1944)
EHC St. Moritz, Switzerland (1933-1934)
Diavoli Rosso Neri, Italy (1934-1936)
SG Eichkamp, Berlin, Germany (1946-1948)
Tigers IHC Johannesburg, South Africa (1949-1950)
Wolves IHC Johannesburg, South Africa (1950-1951)

International:
Germany 49 games – 19 goals

Honors:
Olympic Games (1932-Bronze, 1936)
World Championships (1930-Silver, 1933, 1937, 1938)
European Championship (1929, 1932-Bronze)
German Championship (8 times)
South African Championship (1 time)
Spengler Cup (3 times)
Scoring Leader - German League (10 times)
Lifetime Goals - Over 500
Elected to International Ice Hockey Hall of Fame (2004)

ADDENDUM
A FINAL WORD FROM THE AUTHOR

My wife once told me that I still thought I was a 15 year old, because I wanted to always be playing a game at which I wasn't really all that good. She cannot understand why one would risk injury at my age to participate in a game that requires such physical stamina. Yet, she can sit in the stands with me and get excited watching a bunch of young men play the game. (I wonder if it is hockey she is watching or the young men?)

My wife has a cat she loves dearly, and I am scared which one of us she would pick, if she had to choose between us. However, she has often told me that she is glad that I never had to make a choice between playing a hockey game and getting her to the hospital in an emergency. I always tell her it would depend on how important the game was.

In Canada, there is a national religion – it is called hockey. Being born in and living the first 18 years of my life in North Carolina, I was a bit unusual in my affection for a sport that few southerners played and watched on television. However, my cousin and I were dedicated followers of the sport and spent hours playing the game with brooms for sticks and wadded-up tin foil for a puck. Unfortunately for my dear grandmother, most of the playing was done on her back porch. Needless to say, she was not too sympathetic to our love of a game that constantly kept her wooden back porch scratched up and the screens that surrounded it filled with holes our pucks and elbows made. I remember one time when we tore out a whole section of the porch when I violently checked my cousin through the screen mesh onto the ground outside. That may have been one of my best checks ever. It was also one of the many times that I took advantage of my younger cousin's trusting nature.

Several years ago, just after moving to Canada, I wrote a newspaper article about hockey, and I think it helps sum-up what hockey means to so many of us

CANADIAN HOCKEY - MORE THAN A GAME
by
J. Wayne Frye

When we were youths in the 1950's and 1960's, my cousin Monte and I used to spend lazy winter Saturday afternoons at my grandmother's stately old home in Asheboro, North Carolina glued to the TV set, as two of the Original Six NHL teams battled it out on ice. Watching "Terrible Ted," "The Rocket," "Boom-Boom," "Gordie (Mr. Elbows)," "Bobby" and the "Gumper" in living black and white on the tiny 12 inch screen was the highlight of our week. As helmet-less blurs of sheer energy streaked down the ice in what could only be described as sheer mayhem, we would lean forward and squint our eyes to get a better view of the players whom we idolized while our youthful compatriots were worshipping the wimpy sports heroes of baseball, basketball and football. My cousin and I were two of the few southerners who knew that "real men" played hockey.

Between periods and after the game, we would grab our grandmother's broom and mop to use for hockey sticks, crumble up some tin foil for a puck, and head to her screened-in back porch that measured 12 by 35 to engage in our specialized version of ice hockey. Scratching the grey-painted wooden floor, and occasionally lifting the puck high enough to indent the wire screen made her remind us that she was constantly repainting and re-screening the porch as a result of our fervent hockey extravaganzas. Then, with her hickory stick she used for dipping snuff hanging from the side of her mouth, she would smile, turn and walk away, knowing that the game must go on for two dedicated hockey aficionados who saw hockey as the reason they were born.

In the 1950's and 1960's,there were only two ice-rinks in the entire state of North Carolina, and to this day, I still hold a grudge against my parents for being unwilling to drive the 50 kilometres to a nearby rink at 4:00 AM, so I could play hockey. I played baseball, basketball and football, but they all pale in comparison to the thrill of cold air rising from the ice, blowing in your face as you streak toward that dreaded goalie, ready to challenge his prowess at keeping the round black disc from invading his domain. It is a feeling like no other in the world, and there is no way it can be effectively described. It must be experienced to understand the exhilaration and pure majesty that comes from being on the frozen field of battle where two teams face off in combat.

In 2003, disillusioned with the direction the USA was headed under the leadership of two self-aggrandizing, heartless war mongers who thought all problems could be solved with bombs and bullets and that all the benefits of society should flow to those at the top of the economic ladder, I decided to take early retirement and crossed the border into Canada. One of the proudest moments of my life was when I took the oath of citizenship and genuinely became a Canadian.

Yet, I also discovered something else. In a career as a hockey coach, businessman, professor, TV producer/director and educational administrator; I have lived in eleven different places. However, I always made sure that each place I moved had hockey programs for my children. A few of the moves combined my job as a professor with that of a hockey coach. My final move was to a place where hockey is more than a game. Being a Canadian means that you have a special place in your heart for a sport that is emblematic of what makes Canada the great nation that it is. The game represents liberty to Canadians. We Canadians view the sport as a microcosm of all that makes us who we are.

Life, for most people, is a continuous battle against the forces of political and economic oppression. Most of us are not born with a silver spoon in our mouths. We do not have things handed to us as if we are entitled. That is only reserved for the moneyed class and royalty – the very people who often look with disdain on the rest of us who are relegated to struggling through life since we are afforded no special privileges by virtue of birth.

Hockey is more than a game. It is a battle on ice between an unmovable object and an unstoppable force. The smooth, graceful, rhythmic glide of a skater moving through the arena of combat to confront foes who guard that steel posted mesh-covered fortification brings us all to our feet in awe as bodies litter the ice with the carnage wrought by men determined to be victorious in a battle of iron-willed gladiators. This is why Canadians do not need to flex their muscles to the world. There is no need to impose their will on others. Canadians gloriously reduce their national pride to an 85 feet by 200 feet arena, where for three twenty minute periods a battle of skill, will-power, force and strength is conducted with an unmitigated commitment to winning. Yet, when the smoke of battle has cleared and when the bloody defeated have picked themselves up from the field of battle knowing they gave it their all, and when the victorious minions of combat have triumphantly embraced in harmonious celebration of their conquest; the combatants boldly line-up in mutual reverence to file past, shaking hands as a show of respect. This is the Canadian psyche that makes us all proud to be part of something that defines us as a nation. We can battle furiously for an hour on a sheet of ice, but after the buzzer sounds, all animosity is put aside, our wooden or composite stick weapons are thrown asunder and we embrace in mutual recognition and respect.

My cousin and I communicate regularly by e-mail, and our number one topic of discussion is hockey. Although our political philosophies and religious beliefs are diametrically opposite, we are forever bound together by our mutual respect and love for the grandmother who was such an integral part of our young lives. However, it is hockey that is the thread that reaches beyond time, border and distance to unite us in the mutual understanding of its importance in our past, present and future. I can still fondly recall sliding across my grandmother's grey back porch floor in our stocking feet, mop and broom in hand, battling furiously for control of our tin foil puck, pushing, shoving, checking and even occasionally engaging in a staged fight. I can almost hear her now berating us and then finally giving up and saying, "this hockey stuff is driving an old woman crazy." Oh Canada, let's all get crazy............

Article reprinted with permission from:
Times Courier News Syndicate
Copyright 2007

This is the author, still living in his fantasy world, where the "Knights of the Ice" battle to protect their 4 feet by 6 feet kingdom that lies between two metal posts and a crossbar backed by cloth mesh. (Picture from 2008 at Nanaimo Ice Centre in Nanaimo, BC)

**IF YOU ENJOYED THIS BOOK ABOUT
HOCKEY, READ
*HOCKEY MANIA AND THE MYSTERY OF
NANCY RUNNING ELK*
ALSO BY J. WAYNE FRYE
AVAILABLE AT AMAZON.COM OR YOUR
LOCAL RETAILERS**

The *TO KILL A MOCKINGBIRD* of the 21st Century.

HOCKEY
MANIA
AND THE MYSTERY
OF NANCY RUNNING ELK

J. Wayne Frye

With an Introduction
By
Jasmine Falling Rain Frye

The story of an extraordinary hockey team that defied all
the odds one remarkable season, and a player who solved
a murder and helped a beautiful young member of his tribe
find peace in her troubled life.

CANADIAN ANGELS OF MERCY: NURSES IN TIMES OF PERIL 1885-1918

JASMINE FALLING RAIN FRYE
J. WAYNE FRYE

A harrowing tale of nurses in the Crimean War, Boar War And World War I

PHOTO CREDITS

All photos used are in the public domain,
as original and renewal copyrights have expired.

Page 6: Archives of PCHA
Page 10: Wikipedia
Page 11: Wikipedia
Page 13: Berlin Time Capsule Photos
Page 15: The History Box
Page 16: The History Box
Page 17: On-Line Royalty Free Photos
Page 22: Olympic Archives
Page 24: Sports Almanac
Page 26: Sports Almanac (both photos)
Page 27: Olympic Archives
Page 29: Nuevo Zectung Abbildung
Page 30: Kurier Newspaper Archives
Page 34: German War-Time Internet Photo Gallery
        (Hitler)
        Holocaust Museum Photo Gallery (Jews-Star
        Of David)
Page 35: Holocaust Museum Photo Gallery (both
        pPhotos)
Page 36: Kurier Newspaper Archives
Page 37: Kurier Newspaper Archives (cartoon)
        Holocaust Museum Photo Gallery (Do Not
        Enter)
Page 41: U.S. Civil Rights Museum (both)
Page 44: Olympic Archives
Page 46: Kurier Newspaper Archives
Page 49: National German Sports Archives
Page 54: Kurier Newspaper Archives
Page 60: Olympic Archives

Rudi Ball Bibliographic Information

Researching this book was extremely difficult. Finding relatives of Rudi Ball was next to impossible, as they have scattered all over the world. The South African Hockey Federation, seemed totally bewildered when I mentioned the name Rudi Ball. Even in Germany, where hockey is still the second most popular sport, few people with whom I talked had ever heard of Rudi Ball. Dependent on archival information from a variety of sources did afford me the opportunity to put together the pieces of a perplexing puzzle, but the lack of information was thoroughly frustrating. I must admit to some embellishment to fill in gaps, but the crux of the story is true in regards to the exploits of Rudi Ball. How ironic that a true hockey icon is not better remembered.

I want to express profound gratitude to the U.S. Holocaust Museum which allows the public to access the video exhibits dealing with the 1936 Garish-Partenkirchen and Berlin Olympics in Germany. The International Ice Hockey Hall of Fame was also immensely helpful, as was the Jewish Virtual Library Association. Deidre Klopperman must be thanked for her assistance in German translations. Finally, a very special thanks to my cousin and fellow hockey lover, Monte Cagle, whose editing assistance was invaluable. Furthermore, the following web-sites were particularly helpful in assembling information on Rudi Ball:

http://www.greatesthockeylegends.com
http://www.vhec.org/rudiballbiography.htm
http://www.pipl.com/1936_olympics/pdf/the_1936_game s_

http://www.en.wikipedia.org/wiki/rudyball
http://www.sihss.se/RudiBallbiography.htm
http://www.vhec.org/136_olympics/pdf/the_1936_games_
pdf
http://www.goirpigs.com/?p=6126
http://www.dbedia.org/page/Rudi_Ball
http//www.jewsinsports.org/olympics.asp?ID=222
http:www.WeitereSeiten/zutripatlas.com/rudiball
http:www.WeitereSeiten/forums/internationalicehockey.n
et
http://www.luise-berlin.de/sport/b/be.htm

VOCABULARY FROM PROLOGUE
& CHAPTER 1

[1] Holocaust – great destruction causing an extensive loss of life, specifically refers to genocide (the extermination or near-extermination of a racial, religious or ethnic groups). Common term used for the attempted extermination of all Jews by Germany in World War II.

[1] Camaraderie – trust existing between people, usually friends or team-mates.

[1] Initial – beginning or first.

[1] Prologue – an introduction to a book or event. What comes before.

Emancipation – to be free from bondage or restraint. To liberate.

Perpetrated – to perform or be responsible for something that is done.

Antiquated – too old to be fashionable, suitable or useful.

Metaphor – an implied comparison between two unlike things that have something in common.

Transcends – to pass or go beyond the limits.

Metaphor – an implied comparison between two unlike things that have something in common.

Transcends – to pass or go beyond the limits.

Kaiser – German term for Emperor.

Amenities – things intended for material comfort.

Disparity – lack of similarity or equality, inequality, difference.

Exhilaration – state of being lively, joyful or cheerful.

Animosity – powerful dislike or hostility.

Catapult – launching something. A dramatic conveyance.

Oblivious – unaware or unconcerned in regards to the consequences of something.

Nonchalantly – unconcerned or indifferent. Completing a task with great ease of effort.

Precocious – inquisitive by nature and always looking for mental stimulation.

Lebensraum – German for space.

Prowess – superior skill or ability.

Awe – overwhelming feeling of reverence or admiration.

VOCABULARY FROM CHAPTER 2

Coincided – occurring at or near the same time.

Ironic – contrary to what is expected or intended.

Condemnation – an expression of strong disapproval.

Scapegoat – a person or group made to bear the blame for others or to suffer in their place.

Perennially – continuing without cessation or intermission, perpetual, never ending, unceasing.

Truculent – bitter opposition, fierce.

Illustrious – widely known, conferring glory, held in high esteem.

Annals – historical records.

Discontent – dissatisfaction. Restless longing for better circumstances.

Dire – extreme danger, nearly hopeless, desperate situation, awful risk.

Persecution – attacking people through a variety of means because of their race, religion, gender, sexual orientation or beliefs.

Maladies – an unwholesome or bothersome condition.

Oratorical – related to speaking.

Diminutive – small, tiny, little.

VOCABULARY FROM CHAPTER 3

Severe – causing great discomfort or damage.
Great Depression – world economic collapse caused by
the stock market crash of 1929, in which unemployment
remained high for an extended time-period and businesses
had a large rate of failures.
Electrified – in context of this book, to thrill with a
powerful performance.
Prowess – superior skill or ability
Solidifying – to make strong or united.

VOCABULARY FROM CHAPTER 4

Rev – to accelerate sharply in speed.
Captivating – to attract and hold by charm, beauty or
excellence.
Infamy – infamous (deplorable, bad) act or event.
Deteriorating – to weaken or impair quality.
Turmoil – state of confusion.
Chancellor – German head of government.
Innocuous – harmless.
Reichstag – building where the legislative assembly
meets in Germany.
Fuhrer – German word for leader that has come to
signify a tyrant since Hitler's time in office.
Inexorable – ruthless.
Boycott – to not buy or use.
Star of David – six-pointed star made of two inter-
locking triangles. It is a symbol of Judaism (Jews).
Aryans Only – the Nazis considered the Aryan race (pure
Germans) to be superior to other races, and because of
this, they passed laws excluding "non-Aryans" from full
participation in German society.
Systematically – in a consistent manner or way.

Renowned – widely honored or acclaimed.

Unanimous Consent – approval without a vote, because everyone agrees.

Propaganda – doctrines or principles spread by an organization, movement or political body. The information spread can be used to praise the organization or to attack opponents. Truth is often ignored.

Vilify – to make mean, vicious statements about.

Anti-Semite – prejudice against or hostility toward Jews, often rooted in hatred of their ethnic background, culture and/or religion.

Stellar – outstanding.

Indoctrinating – to instil with a specific view.

Fatherland – a person's native land, particularly relevant to WW II Germany.

Sieg Heil – German phrase that means "hail victory."

VOCABULARY FROM CHAPTER 5

Consolidation – a merger of two or more things. A bringing together.

Plethora – an abundance or excess.

Purge – to get rid of something or to eliminate.

Judenrein – German for cleansed of Jews.

Cower – to cringe in fear.

Confiscated – to take from or seize.

Hypocritical – a person who publicly supports certain moral values, but in private ignores those values.

Decried – to openly condemn or voice disapproval.

Furor – commotion, disorder or uproar.

Acquiesced – to consent or comply. To agree to do something.

Persecution – to attack someone because of race, gender, sexual orientation or beliefs that are different from the individual who is engaged in the actual persecuting.

Exile – enforced or self-imposed absence from one's country.

Calamity – an event that brings terrible loss, a disaster.

Emigrate – leaving one country to take up permanent residence in another (the opposite of immigrate, which is going to a country – you emigrate from and immigrate to)

Concentration-camp – a place of harsh conditions where people are confined.

Hierarchy – government by an elite group. Individual rankings in a group.

Resigned – to accept as inevitable, to submit.

Disdain – strong dislike, to consider something beneath you.

Menace – a possible danger or threat.

Engulfing – to swallow up or overwhelm.

Plague – a widespread affliction or calamity. A sudden destructive outbreak.

VOCABULARY FROM CHAPTER 6

Promulgate – to put into effect or make known.

Absurd – ridiculous, not reasonable.

Ethnicity – the ethnic (racial, religious) group to which one belongs.

Defying – opposing or resisting with boldness.

Third Reich – the Germany of 1933-1945 under the rule of Hitler (actual German translation is "The Third Empire").

Foremost – first in time, place or rank.

Imbuing – instilling or inspiring with ideas and principles.

Ideologies – a set of ideas that comes from a group, class or culture.
Supplanted – to displace or substitute (sometimes in underhanded fashion).
Mayhem – violent disorder or confusion.
Fisticuffs – activity of fighting with fists.
Altercations – an angry discussion, argument or quarrel that can be physical.
Integrity – following a strict moral or ethical code.
Imbuing – instilling or inspiring with ideas and principles.
Ideologies – a set of ideas that comes from a group, class or culture.
Supplanted – to displace or substitute (sometimes in underhanded fashion).
Mayhem – violent disorder or confusion.
Fisticuffs – activity of fighting with fists.
Altercations – an angry discussion, argument or quarrel that can be physical.
Integrity – following a strict moral or ethical code.
Handily – in an easy manner.
Feisty – full of spirit, frisky or spunky.
Handily – in an easy manner.
Feisty – full of spirit, frisky or spunky.
Titanic – of enormous stature, scope, strength or importance.
Palette – a board with a hole for the thumb to hold an artist's paints.
Refuge – protection or shelter from hardship or danger.
Tempest – furious agitation, commotion or uproar.
Perpetrated – to be responsible for (deception, crime or an idea).
Condemnation – strong disapproval or judgment against something.

Anguish – agonizing physical or mental pain; torment.
Essence – crucial element; the unchanging nature of a thing.
Flittered – to flutter (less common use of the term flutter).
Confounding – to cause or become confused.
Prowess – superior skill or ability.
Deft – quick, nimble, skillful in movement.
Unison – at the same time (all together).
Apprehensive – uneasy, fearful or anxious about something.
Hallmark – quality or excellence.
Archrival – a principal rival. A particularly fierce competitor.
Oppression – cruel exercise of power over someone or a group.
Despotism – absolute power or authority.
Sanctity – something considered sacred or holy.

VOCABULARY FROM CHAPTER 7

Comprehend – to understand.
Intervene – to come between two things. Something unusual interrupts.
Quarter – to show no mercy or clemency to an enemy or rival (in this book, it refers to neither team being willing to give-in, no matter what the costs).
Vanquished – to defeat or conquer in battle.
Endeavour – an attempt to do something.
Excruciating – intensely painful, agonizing, very intense, extreme.
Adamant – stubborn or unyielding.
Despondent – dejected, downtrodden or deeply concerned.

Deteriorate – to weaken.
Reverberated – repeating (sound waves), rebounding sounds.
Skittering – to move rapidly along a surface, usually with direction changes.
Chaos – disorder and confusion.
Summersault – the complete revolution of the body knees tucked in and the feet coming over the head.
Artistry – artistic ability.
Pandemonium – wild uproar, usually accompanied by loud noise.
Marvel – amazing, admirable or utterly surprising.
Supplication – to humble yourself before another person.

VOCABULARY FROM EPILOGUE

Epilogue – a concluding part of a literary work.
Lacerated – ripped, torn, mangled or cut.
Laden – heavy with. (In this case, the British team had 10 of its 12 players from Canada.)
Seething – to be in a high state of turmoil or anger.
Deprivation – great loss, deprived of something necessary.
Revered – to hold in high regard.
Devastation – to lay waste, destroy, overwhelm.
Valiant – bravely done with valor.
Prodigious – wonderful or amazing.
Deprivation – great loss, deprived of something necessary.
Revered – to hold in high regard.
Devastation – to lay waste, destroy, overwhelm.
Valiant – bravely done with valor.
Prodigious – wonderful or amazing.

Lured – to tempt or attract.
Epitaph – an inscription on a tombstone in memory of someone buried there.
Posthumously – occurring or continuing after one's death.
Intimidating – to fill with fear.
Pettiness – meanness or lack of generosity.

CHAPTER QUESTIONS

Prologue

1. Interpret the meaning of the poem by Ryan Frye.
2. How does the poem by Ryan Frye describe hockey as it in terms of his relationship with his dad?
3. Why is hockey described as "a war" by the author?
4. What does the author say about being a loser?
5. Describe how the author feels about losing the championship game. How can you relate hockey in this instance to every day life?
6. Why do you think the author spends time discussing hockey in general when the story is mostly about one player (Rudi Ball)?

Chapter 1

1. Describe the Berlin of Rudy's youth.
2. What was the biggest industry in Berlin at the time and how were workers treated?
3. Describe Rudy's family and their economic status.
4. What was the biggest economic problem of the time?
5. Why was the Social Democratic party so important?
6. What was the leader of Germany called at this time?
7. What incident led to World War I?
8. Who was Germany's ally in World War I?
9. How did the people feel about the war at first?
10. Who owned most of the newspapers in Germany at this time?
11. Describe how people got food during the war, and what did they eat?
12. What was the treaty that ended the war called?
13. Discuss the guilt clause in the treaty.

14. What economic malady made Germany fall into chaos?
15. Describe Rudi's physical looks when he was a small child.
16. Describe Rudi's relationship with his mother.
17. Describe how the Jews were treated after Germany's defeat in World War I.
18. What political party was formed in 1919 and who eventually became its leader?
19. What book did Hitler write while he was in jail and what was its purpose?
20. Name and discuss the four things Hitler advocated in his book.
21. What did some people use for fires after World War I?
22. At what age did Rudi start playing hockey seriously?
23. What did most players use for pucks in those days?
24. Why did Rudi value his skates so much?
25. What nickname did one sports official give Rudi?

Chapter 2

1. What did Rudi's rise as a hockey player coincide with?
2. What was unique about the three best hockey players in Germany at the time?
3. What is a tried and true method to get people to support your cause? (It was used in Germany and many other countries to get people to support a cause. Can you name a recent example when it was used to rally people to a cause.)
4. What are most real problem actually caused by?
5. Name two things unique about the Berliner SC team?
6. What happened in 1929 when Rudi was 18?
7. What great friend played with Rudi in 1929?

8. What was happening in regards to unemployment in Germany at this time, and how could that help the Nazis?
9. What was unusual about the 1930 World Ice Hockey Championships?
10. What happened to the Canadian for the first time in 1930?
11. How were hockey teams of those days different from today's hockey teams?
12. Rudi was known as what when it came to playing time?

Chapter 3

1. How did one newspaper describe the 1931-1932 season?
2. What make the 1932 Winter Olympics in lake Placid lose some of their lustre?
3. What was unique about the German Bronze medal in 1932?

Chapter 4

1. How did one goalie describe Rudi?
2. As Rudi's reputation grew who else's reputation was also soaring?
3. What honour was bestowed on Gerhard Ball in the 1932-1933 season?
4. What dramatic event occurred in 1933 off-the-ice that would have profound implications for Rudi?
5. What caused the Enabling Act to be passed?
6. What was the Enabling Act?
7. What new political office was created?
8. What other groups besides the Jews were singled out for persecution?

9. Discuss the specific anti-Jewish laws that prevented them from doing certain things.
10. The Nazi Sports Office instituted what policy in 1933?
11. Rudi was allowed to keep playing for the German team during these years, and when asked about why he played when there was so much prejudice against Jews what was his reply?
12. What were individual Jews and Jewish owned businesses forced to do starting in 1934 to identify themselves?
13. What influential group did the Nazis bombard with propaganda to convince them to hate Jews?
14. Who did the Nazis blamed for the death of Jesus?
15. Who had to approve school books in Germany?
16. What did all school children have to do before the beginning of every school day?

Chapter 5

1. In 1936 something happened for the only time in history. What was it?
2. What does Judenrein mean?
3. What one main idea was Hitler obsessed with?
4. What did Hitler think the Olympics offered him a chance to prove?
5. To Hitler, sports was an opportunity to reduce sports to what?
6. Why argument did the Germans use against the Americans when they wanted to boycott the winter games?
7. What argument did Joseph Goebbles use against the Americans in regards to confiscating land?
8. What American was considered a Nazi sympathizer?

9. What did one American say about why there were no Jews on the German teams?

10. Newspapers in Germany used what examples to attack what they termed American hypocrisy?

11. Why did Great Britain and the USA want to make sure Canada did not boycott the games?

12. What was unique about the British ice hockey team?

13. What did the German team do when Rudi was not selected for the 1936 Olympic team?

14. What was the personal reason that made Rudi want to play on the team?

15. What final step taken by the German team outraged the Nazis?

Chapter 6

1. As a Jew, what did Rudi think he was proving by playing for the German team?

2. Who did Hitler think would be the real star of the games?

3. What was unique about the Canadian Olympic team?

4. How did the Nazis view sports?

5. What thinks often supplanted sportsmanship at the Olympics?

6. Why was hockey considered unique among sports?

7. What did the German players think was more important than Nazi ideology?

8. What was interesting about the Olympic salute as this time?

9. One journalist described Rudi as being similar to a what?

10. Describe Rudi's speech to his team before the game against Hungary.

11. To whom were the German players devoted?

12. What did each player seem to be saying to Hitler when they skated onto the ice?

Chapter 7

1. What does fate sometimes make us?
2. The game against Hungary was more than just a game. It was a what?
3. These players looked on the hockey rink as a field of what?
4. When are losers not really losers?
5. Describe how Rudi felt about love?
6. What happened to Rudi in the first period of the game against Hungary?
7. Discuss the poem, *There is Blood on the Battlefield*, and what it means.

Epilogue

1. What happened when Germany played Great Britain?
2. How did the Canadians approach the game against the Germans?
3. While Rudi was struggling to bring a medal to Germany, what was going on outside the rink?
4. What happened to Rudi during the war?
5. What did Rudi do between 1945 and 1948?
6. What did Rudi decide to do in 1948?
7. What was Rudi's reply when a journalist said that hockey owed him more recognition than he had received?
8. Name some of the honours Rudi received.

Addendum

1. What is considered a national religion in Canada?

2. What did Monte and Wayne use for hockey sticks?
3. Why does the author still hold a grudge against his parents?
4. What was one of the proudest moments of the suthor's life?
5. Why do Canadians not have to "flex their muscles to the world?"
6. What unites the author and his cousin?

REFERENCES FOR 1936 OLYMPICS
FOR FURTHER STUDY
(Retrieved From)
http://www.ushmm.org/research/library/bibliography/
index.php?content=1936_olympics

- Eisen, George. "The Voices of Sanity: American Diplomatic Reports from the 1936 Berlin Olympiad." *Journal of Sport History* 11, no. 3 (1984): 56-78. (Subject Files) [Find in a library near you]
  Reviews the confidential diplomatic reports from key American officials in Germany in the years leading up to the Games: the American ambassador, William E. Dodd; consul general, George S. Messersmith; and consul, Raymond H. Geist. Recounts their observations of rising antisemitism in Germany in the mid-1930s and their diplomatic proposals for how the U.S. should approach the Olympics and the boycott movement.

- Kieran, John, and Arthur Daley. *The Story of the Olympic Games: 776 B.C. to 1964.* Philadelphia: Lippincott, 1965. (GV 23 .K5 1965) [Find in a library near you]
  Reviews the history of the Olympics from ancient Greece to the modern Olympic movement. Provides a chapter on each of the Summer

Olympiads from 1896 to 1964, including Berlin in 1936.

- Krüger, Arnd, and Murray, William, editors. *The Nazi Olympics: Sport, Politics and Appeasement in the 1930s*. Urbana: University of Illinois Press, 2003. (GV 722 1936 .N389 2003) [Find in a library near you]
  Collection of essays exploring how the Nazi Party used the 1936 Olympics as a stage for political maneuvering among the participating countries. Individual essays outline the ways political and military interests of the time affected the Games. Includes a bibliographic essay and index.

- Krüger, Arnd. "'Once the Olympics are through, we'll beat up the Jew': German Jewish Sport 1898-1938 and the Anti-Semitic Discourse." *Journal of Sport History* 26, No. 2 (1999): 353-375. (Subject Files) [Find in a library near you]
  Article outlining the development of Jewish participation in German athletic clubs in the early 20th century, and how these organizations were affected by the rise of the Nazi party in the 1930s.

- Mandell, Richard D. *The Nazi Olympics*. Urbana: University of Illinois Press, 1987. (GV 722 1936 M3 1987) [Find in a library near you]
  Examines the historical framework of the 1936

Olympics within the context of German attitudes towards sport and individual competition. Summarizes the political atmosphere of Germany in 1936 and the jingoistic and propagandistic purposes to which the Games were put by the Nazi leadership.

- Miller, Patrick B. "The Nazi Olympics, Berlin, 1936: Exhibition at the U.S. Holocaust Memorial Museum, Washington, D.C." *Olympika: The International Journal of Olympic Studies* 5 (1996): 127-139. (Subject Files) [Find in a library near you]
Review of the exhibit "The Nazi Olympics: Berlin 1936," on display at the United States Holocaust Memorial Museum in 1996-1997. Comments on the prominent themes of the exhibit, such as the movement within the United States to boycott the Games and the impact of Nazism on Jewish athletes from around the world, as well as the continuing impact of these events on the relationship between politics and sport.

- Murray, W.J. "France, Coubertin and the Nazi Olympics: The Response." *Olympika: The International Journal of Olympic Studies* 1 (1992): 46-69. (Subject Files) [Find in a library near you]
Reconstructs the controversy surrounding a 1936 editorial in the French sports journal L'Auto

which decried the Games as "défigurés" ("disfigured") by Nazism, and the impassioned defense of the Games by the founder of the modern Olympics, Pierre de Frédy, Baron de Coubertin. Reviews the discussions in the French press of the role of nationalism and racism in the Games. Includes extensive endnotes.

The Boycott Movement

- Committee on Fair Play in Sports. *Preserve the Olympic Ideal: A Statement of the Case Against American Participation in the Olympic Games at Berlin.* New York: The Committee, 1935. (GV 722 1936 C6 1935) [Find in a library near you] A booklet written in response to the American Olympic Committee's defense of participation in the 1936 Olympics in face of the grass roots boycott movement. Outlines the discriminatory conditions faced by German Jewish athletes and provides examples of the outward manifestations of German anti-Semitism found in public signs.

- Gray, Wendy. "Devotion to Whom?: German-American Loyalty on the Issue of Participation in the 1936 Olympic Games." *Journal of Sport History* 17, no. 2 (1990): 214-231. (Subject Files) [Find in a library near you]

Examines the actions and possible motivations of various German-American organizations, including the Bund, who were particularly ardent in their support for American involvement in the 1936 Olympics in face of mounting criticism of the Nazi government and calls to boycott the Games. Includes an appendix listing the stated "Purpose and Aims" of the German American Bund.

- Guttmann, Allen. "The 'Nazi Olympics' and the American Boycott Controversy." In *Sport and International Politics: The Impact of Fascism and Communism on Sport*, edited by Pierre Arnaud and James Riordan, 47-62. New York: E & FN Spon, 1998. (GV 706.35 .S58 1998) [Find in a library near you]
Explores the political framework of the boycott movement in the United States in its attempts to sway Avery Brundage, the head of the American Olympic Committee, against American participation in the Berlin Games. Summarizes contemporary opinion in the American press concerning the Games.

- Kass, D.A. "The Issue of Racism at the 1936 Olympics." *Journal of Sport History* 3, no. 3 (1976): 223-235. (Subject Files) [Find in a library near you]

Describes the arguments for and against the possible U.S. boycott of the Games that were prompted by Germany's racial doctrines and laws.

- Lipstadt, Deborah E. "The Olympic Games: Germany Triumphant." In *Beyond Belief: The American Press and the Coming of the Holocaust, 1933-1945*, 63-85. New York: Free Press, 1986. (DS 135 .G33 L57 1986) [Find in a library near you]
Analyzes the American press reaction to the movement to boycott the Berlin Olympics that was active in the United States from 1933 to 1936. Reviews the diverse opinions in the press regarding the Nazi regime vis-à-vis the ideals of the Olympic movement. Also describes the media coverage of the propaganda spectacle of the 1936 Olympic ceremonies and events. Based on contemporary newspaper articles and the correspondence of officials from the American Olympic Committee and the State Department.

- Swanson, Richard A. "'Move the Olympics!' 'Germany Must Be Told!': Charles Clayton Morrison and Liberal Protestant Christianity's Support of the 1936 Olympic Boycott Effort." *Olympika* 12 (2003): 39-50. (Subject Files) [Find in a library near you]
Documents the efforts of Charles Clayton

Morrison's journal *The Christian Century* to pressure the U.S. to either press for the Games to be moved from Nazi Germany or for the U.S. to boycott the 1936 Olympics entirely.

- Wenn, Stephen R. "A Tale of Two Diplomats: George S. Messersmith and Charles H. Sherrill on Proposed American Participation in the Berlin Olympics." *Journal of Sport History* 16, no. 1 (1989): 27-43. (Subject Files) [Find in a library near you]
  Article detailing the roles played by two men--U.S. Consul General George S. Messersmith and the American representative to the International Olympic Committee, Charles H. Sherrill--in the process behind the decision by the United States to participate in the 1936 Games.

The Games

- Bachrach, Susan D. *The Nazi Olympics: Berlin 1936*. Boston: Little, Brown, 2000. (GV 722 1936 B27 2000) [Find in a library near you]
  Provides a comprehensive narrative of the 1936 Games with an emphasis on the international political reaction to the Nazi policies regarding Jewish athletes. Includes biographical sidebars on many participants, banned athletes, and

boycotters. Based on the 1996 United States Holocaust Memorial Museum exhibition of the same name and intended for a juvenile audience.

- Cohen, Stan. *The Games of '36: A Pictorial History of the 1936 Olympics in Germany.* Missoula, MT: Pictorial Histories Publishing, 1996. (GV 722 1936 C678 1996) [Find in a library near you]
Chronicles the Games in Berlin and Garmisch-Partenkirchen through reproductions of contemporary photographs, documents and newspaper stories. Provides capsule biographies of many of the noteworthy athletes and organizers of the Games.

- Constable, George, et al. *The XI, XII & XIII Olympiads: Berlin 1936, St. Moritz 1948.* Los Angeles: World Sport Research & Publications, 1996. (Oversize GV 722 1936 C65 1996) [Find in a library near you]
Recounts the history of the Berlin Games through narrative, event schedules and event results. Also provides a narrative of the events surrounding the cancellation of the 1940 Olympics and the suspension of the Olympic Games through the rest of the war years.

- Graham, Cooper C. *Leni Riefenstahl and Olympia.* Lanham, MD: Scarecrow Press, 2001. (GV 722 1936 .G73 2001) [Find in a library near you] Recounts the creation and subsequent history of *Olympia*, Leni Riefenstahl's documentary about the Berlin Olympic Games. Examines the technical challenges involved in filming Olympic events and the controversy engendered by the filmmaker's relationship with the Nazi regime. Provides English translations of a selection of documents concerning the history of the film, including the production contract between Riefenstahl and the Reich Ministry of Propaganda. Includes a bibliography, an index, and numerous photographs of Riefenstahl and her crew taken during the making of the film.

- Guttmann, Allen, Heather Kestner, and George Eisen. "Jewish Athletes and the 'Nazi Olympics.'" In *The Olympics at the Millennium: Power, Politics, and the Games*, edited by Kay Schaffer and Sidonie Smith, 51-62. New Brunswick, NJ: Rutgers University Press, 2000. (GV 721.5 .O425 2000) [Find in a library near you] Summarizes the treatment of Jewish athletes at the 1936 Games.

- Hart-Davis, Duff. *Hitler's Games: The 1936 Olympics.* New York: Harper & Row, 1986. (GV

The Rudi Ball Story   121

722 1936 H37 1986) [Find in a library near you] Examines the organization of the Berlin Games in terms of their display of a renewed German militarism and their propagandistic value for the Nazi regime. Includes a chart listing all the medal winners at the Summer Olympiad.

- Hilton, Christopher. *Hitler's Olympics: The 1936 Berlin Olympic Games*. Stroud: Sutton, 2006. (GV 722 1936 .H55 2006) [Find in a library near you] Considers events leading up the Games including the initial German bid to make Berlin the host city and the political atmosphere in Germany at the time. Recounts daily events during the Games, incorporating numerous personal accounts. Includes photographs, a bibliography, and statistics for all medal winners.

- Holmes, Judith. *Olympiad 1936: Blaze of Glory for Hitler's Reich*. New York: Ballantine, 1971. (GV 722 1936 H65 1971) [Find in a library near you] Explores the history of the 1936 Games, highlighting the Nazi regime's use of the events for propaganda purposes. Includes a historical and critical analysis of *Olympia*, Leni Riefenstahl's film about the Games. Part of a series of illustrated histories of 20th century events.

- Keys, Barbara J. "Between Nazism and Olympism: Berlin, 1936." In *Globalizing Sport: National Rivalry and International Community in the 1930s*, 134-157. Cambridge, MA: Harvard University Press, 2006. (GV 706.34 .K48 2006) [Find in a library near you] Analyzes Nazi efforts to use the Berlin Games as an international forum to demonstrate the efficiency and authority of the Third Reich. Provides an evaluation of the extent to which the 1936 Olympics were tainted by "Nazification."

- Lambert, Margaret Bergmann. *By Leaps and Bounds*. Washington, DC: U.S. Holocaust Memorial Museum, 2005. (DS 135 .G5 B46413 2005) [Find in a library near you] Recounts the author's experiences as a Jewish athlete banned from participating in the 1936 Olympics, her subsequent escape from Germany, and her eventual return trip to that country many years later. Includes photographs.

- Large, David Clay. *Nazi Games: The Olympics of 1936*. New York: W.W. Norton, 2007. (GV722 1936 .L37 2007) [Find in a library near you] Comprehensive history of the 1936 Olympics that considers both the athletic competitions as well as the political climate under which the Games were held. Analyzes Nazi efforts to use the Games as a propaganda event as typified by Leni Riefenstahl's film *Olympia*. Includes numerous photographs of the events and pageantry, extensive notes, and an epilogue evaluating the place of the Games in the overall history of Nazi Germany.

- Riefenstahl, Leni. *Olympia: The Film of the XI Olympic Games* [DVD]. Venice, CA: Pathfinder Home Entertainment, 1938, c2006. (Video Collection) [Find in a library near you] A two-part documentary film about the Berlin Games created by the most well-known German film director of the Nazi era. Chronicles such events as the marathon, the diving competition, and many of the track and field events with innovative camera techniques. Critically acclaimed as a celebration of the human body in motion but also viewed as propagandistic by some critics. The DVD set includes more than five hours of extra materials, including delted scenes and two Nazi-era documentaries that utilized footage from Reifenstahl's film.

- Rippon, Anton. *Hitler's Olympics: The Story of the 1936 Nazi Games*. Barnsley, South Yorkshire: Pen & Sword, 2006. (GV 722 1936 .R57 2006) [Find in a library near you] Comprehensive, journalistic narrative of the planning and realization of the Summer and

Winter Olympics, with particular emphasis on Nazi use of the Games as a propaganda tool. Heavily-illustrated with images from events and ceremonies. Includes a list of sources and an index.

- Rubien, Frederick W., editor. *Report of the American Olympic Committee: Games of the XIth Olympiad, Berlin, Germany, August 1-16, 1936: IVth Olympic Winter Games, Garmisch-Partenkirchen, Germany, February 6-16, 1936.* New York: American Olympic Committee, 1936. (Rare GV 722 1936) [Find in a library near you] Relates the official story of the United States' participation in the 1936 Olympics. Includes statements by Avery Brundage, Frederick Rubien and other American Olympic officials that reflect their generally favorable impression of the Nazi regime and its organization of the Games. Features portraits of many Olympic team members and officials.

- Rürup, Reinhard. *1936, die Olympischen Spiele und der Nationalsozialismus: eine Dokumentation = 1936, the Olympic Games and National Socialism: A Documentation.* Berlin: Stiftung Topographie des Terrors veröffentlicht im Argon Verlag, 1996. (GV 722 1936 A14 1996) [Find in a library near you]

A bilingual exhibition catalogue that recounts the history of the Berlin Games using photographs and reproductions of contemporary documents. Includes a chapter on the "Nazification" of German sports organizations that began in 1933.

- Sant, Christine Duerksen. "'Genuine German Girls:' The Nazi Portrayal of its Sportswomen of the 1936 Berlin Olympics." M.A. Thesis. Wake Forest University, 2000. (GV 709.18 G3 S36 2000) [Find in a library near you]
  A thesis that addresses the Nazi regime's ambivalent attitude towards Germany's female Olympians in the 1936 Games and recounts how the German media portrayed them to the public. Shows how the Third Reich's aspirations to portray Germany's athletic and racial superiority conflicted with its anti-feminist ideology that sought to limit women's roles outside of the domestic setting.

- Walters, Guy. *Berlin Games: How the Nazis Stole the Olympic Dream.* New York: William Morrow, 2006. (GV 722 1936 .W35 2006) [Find in a library near you]
  Uses first-person accounts of athletes, politicians, and Olympic officials to provide an overview history of the events leading up to and during the 1936 Olympics. Reveals how the Nazis subverted

Olympic ideals to project their own political and racial agenda on the Games. Includes numerous photographs, a bibliography, and an index.

Biographies

- Baker, William J. *Jesse Owens: An American Life.* New York: Free Press, 1988. (GV 697.09 .B35 1988) [Find in a library near you] Profiles the life story of the most noted participant in the 1936 Olympics with an emphasis on Owens' struggles against racial discrimination. Includes an examination of the myth surrounding Owens' supposed snubbing by Adolf Hitler at the Berlin Games.

- Glickman, Marty. *The Fastest Kid on the Block: The Marty Glickman Story.* Syracuse, NY: Syracuse University Press, 1996. (GV 1061.15 .G55 A3 1996) [Find in a library near you] A memoir chronicling Glickman's athletic and broadcasting careers while concentrating on his experiences as a member of the United States track and field team of 1936. Recounts the infamous scratching from the 400 meter relay team of Glickman and Sam Stoller, a fellow Jewish-American athlete, by American Olympic officials just prior to the event final.

- Jacobson, Louis. "Herman Goldberg: Baseball Olympian and Jewish-American." In *Baseball History 3: An Annual of Original Baseball Research*, edited by Peter Levine, 71-88. Westport, CT: Meckler, 1990. (GV 862.5 .B37 1990) [Find in a library near you] Relates the life story of a catcher for the 1936 Olympic baseball team that, competing as a demonstration sport, played an exhibition in front of the largest crowd to see a baseball game up until that time. Provides the subject's reminiscences of the atmosphere of Berlin and its Olympic Village in 1936.

- Mogulof, Milly. *Foiled: Hitler's Jewish Olympian: The Helene Mayer Story*. Oakland, CA: RDR Books, 2002. (GV 1144.2 .M39 M64 2002) [Find in a library near you] Biography of Helene Mayer, winner of the gold medal in fencing at the 1928 Olympics, who was allowed to compete as the "token Jewish Olympian" on the German team after a boycott threat pressured the Nazi government to allow her to compete. Includes numerous photographs, a chronology of Mayer's life, endnotes, and a bibliography.

- Schaap, Jeremy. *Triumph: The Untold Story of Jesse Owens and Hitler's Olympics*. Boston:

Houghton Mifflin, 2007. (GV 697 .O9 S33 2007)
[Find in a library near you]
Detailed biography of Jesse Owens that focuses on
his experiences during the 1936 Games. Includes
photographs, endnotes, and an index.

Web Resources

- *Steven Spielberg Film and Video Archive:
  Olympics (Berlin 1936)*
  Presents archival film footage of the Games held
  by the Steven Spielberg Film and Video Archive
  at the United States Holocaust Memorial Museum,
  including sporting events and newsreels of the
  opening ceremonies.

- *The Nazi Olympics: Berlin 1936*
  An online exhibition prepared by the United States
  Holocaust Memorial Museum that tells the story
  of the Berlin Olympiad, concurrent events, and
  their political implications. Features numerous
  photographs, promotional posters and original
  documents.

- *Official Olympic Reports*
  Presented by the Amateur Athletic Foundation of
  Los Angeles. Digital collection of all Official
  Olympic Reports published by the organizing

committees for each of the Games, including downloadable PDF versions of the reports from the 1936 Berlin Olympiad, Volume 1 and Volume 2. Provides detailed listings of the results and organizational aspects of the Games.

Additional Resources

- *Subject Files*
  Ask at the reference desk to see the following subject files for newspaper and periodical articles:
  - "Jewish athletes"
  - "Olympics 1936"

- *Subject Headings*
  To search library catalogUEs or other electronic search tools for materials on the 1936 Olympics, use the following Library of Congress subject headings to retrieve the most relevant citations:
  - Jewish athletes
  - Jewish athletes--Germany
  - Jewish athletes--United States--Biography
  - National socialism and sports
  - Olympics
  - Olympic Games (11th : 1936 : Berlin, Germany)

OTHER BOOKS BY J. WAYNE FRYE

FROM PINE HILL PRESS
The Loss of The American Dream
FROM PYRAMID PRESS
The Fall From Apocalypse
FROM FIRESIDE BOOKS
Cataclysmic Dreams in Black and White
The Catastrophic Calamities of a Village Idiot
Fighting for Justice in the Land of Hypocrisy
Armageddon Now
Something Evil in the Darkness at Hopkins House
Worth
When Jesus Came to Jersey as the Son of Thunder
The Girl Who Stirred Up the Whirlwind
Canadian Angels of Mercy: Nurses in Times of Peril
(With Jasmine H. Frye)
Hockey Mania and the Mystery of Nancy Running Elk
FROM UNIVERSITY PRESS
Introduction to Advertising
Promotions Workbook
Mastering Marketing Research
Advertising Design
Advertising Lab Manual
Guide to Local Radio and Television Copywriting
Marketing Plan Work Book
Public Relations Workbook
FROM EDUCATIONAL RESEARCH ASSOCIATES
Guide to Alternative Education (13 Editions)
How Hockey Saved a Jew From the Holocaust:
The Rudi Ball Story